Sexual Harassment

Sexual Harassment

An Introduction to the Conceptual and Ethical Issues

KEITH DROMM

♦ BROADVIEW GUIDES TO ♦

Business *and* Professional Ethics

broadview press

LIBRARY AND ARCHIVES CANADA CATALOGUING IN PUBLICATION

Dromm, Keith
      Sexual harassment : an introduction to the conceptual and ethical issues / Keith Dromm.

(Broadview guides to business and professional ethics)
Includes bibliographical references and index.
ISBN 978-1-55481-010-9

     1. Sexual harassment. 2. Sexual harassment—Prevention.
3. Business ethics. I. Title. II. Series: Broadview guides to business and professional ethics

HF5549.5.S45D76 2012   658.3'145   C2012-900360-3

BROADVIEW PRESS is an independent, international publishing house, incorporated in 1985.

We welcome comments and suggestions regarding any aspect of our publications—please feel free to contact us at the addresses below or at broadview@broadviewpress.com.

NORTH AMERICA
Post Office Box 1243
Peterborough, Ontario
Canada K9J 7H5

2215 Kenmore Ave.
Buffalo, New York, USA 14207
TEL: (705) 743-8990
FAX: (705) 743-8353

customerservice@broadviewpress.com

UK, EUROPE, CENTRAL ASIA, MIDDLE EAST, AFRICA, INDIA, AND SOUTHEAST ASIA
Eurospan Group, 3 Henrietta St., London WC2E 8LU, United Kingdom
TEL: 44 (0) 1767 604972 FAX: 44 (0) 1767 601640
eurospan@turpin-distribution.com

AUSTRALIA AND NEW ZEALAND
NewSouth Books
c/o TL Distribution, 15-23 Helles Ave.,
Moorebank, NSW, Australia 2170
TEL: (02) 8778 9999 FAX: (02) 8778 9944
orders@tldistribution.com.au

www.broadviewpress.com

Broadview Press acknowledges the financial support of the Government of Canada through the Canada Book Fund for our publishing activities.

Edited by Martin Boyne
Typesetting by Em Dash Design

 This book is printed on paper containing 100% post-consumer fibre.

Printed in Canada

For my students

Contents

Acknowledgments

I have been teaching, studying, and writing about the topic of sexual harassment for several years, and so there are many people from throughout these years to thank for their guidance and inspiration. Christopher Griffin read a very early version of Chapter Four; I thank him for his generosity in reading and commenting on it. My interest in the topic of sexual harassment began when I was teaching courses on the philosophy of love and became interested in ethical issues related to romantic and sexual relationships. I want to thank my students in those classes, in particular students in my Philosophy in Literature course in the fall of 1999 and several sections of Philosophy of Love in subsequent semesters at Northern Arizona University. Students in a variety of courses at the Louisiana Scholars' College and Northwestern State University continue to inspire and challenge me. This book is dedicated to all of my students.

I thank an anonymous reviewer for Broadview Press for helpful suggestions on an earlier draft, and Alex Sager for his invaluable editorial guidance and patience. Finally, I thank Heather Salter Dromm for our conversations about this book and the innumerable other ways in which she supported my writing it.

Introduction

Sexual harassment training is a common event in many workplaces today, with more than 90 per cent of businesses running some form of it (Dolezalek). Despite its prevalence, however, it is for many employees an unpleasant experience. Not only do employees typically dislike it, but many also resent being compelled to undergo such training.

The reasons for these attitudes are probably various. Compulsory training of any sort implies that the trainee *needs* to be improved in some way, and training in the topic of sexual harassment implies that there is some failing in the employees' interpersonal skills. We are probably more sensitive to criticisms of our abilities to interact with others than we are to any other set of skills we might possess. The nature of the training might also offend; sexual harassment training is typically instituted because it is mandated by the law or as a form of protection against lawsuits. If either of these is its only motivation, then the training will likely be perfunctory, simplistic, and even patronizing. It may not be taken seriously by participants, and the trainers, who themselves are obligated to perform the training, might also fail to take it seriously. Failure to take the training seriously can be a response to its poor design and implementation, but many react this way because they believe that the problem of sexual harassment is overblown or not even a problem. Poor training will do little to change this attitude.

One of my own experiences at a sexual harassment training session confirmed some of this. The training was mandated for all employees and required hours from our schedule during a busy time of the year. One of the male presenters began by telling a joke: "I have been trying for years to get someone to sexually harass me, but with no luck." The least of the joke's problems was its unoriginality; in my research for this book I have read reports of its being told at other such training sessions. I know it caused others besides me to resent that time was being taken from our busy schedules for an activity that not even the presenters were taking seriously. However, the worst of the joke's problems is the offense it likely caused to many members of the audience, especially those who have been victims of sexual harassment. There was nothing else in the session that was able to redeem it. Later, when the presenters were asked by an audience member for a definition of sexual harassment, none was able to provide her with a concise, useful answer. So the attendees were left with their understanding of something that should be central to training on sexual harassment—the *meaning* of the term "sexual harassment"—unimproved.

Since my experience in sexual harassment training, I have sometimes wondered how I would approach it if I was ever asked to run a training session on sexual harassment. I have never done so, but I teach the topic in college classes, and I think and write about it academically. But I have thought about how to present what I know about sexual harassment in a professional setting in which what I had to say might have some immediate practical effects. This book is not a consequence of these reflections, and it should not be mistaken for a training manual on sexual harassment. Its goals and orientation are in important ways different. Nevertheless, it does share certain core ideals with my hypothetical sexual harassment training for employees, and I do explore the issue of such training in the final chapter.

First, this book explores the *meaning* of sexual harassment. It begins with this topic in Chapter One: "What is Sexual Harassment?" The chapter starts with a review of the history of both the phenomenon of sexual harassment and the term "sexual harassment." As we will see, the former has a long history but the latter a relatively brief one. I then examine the various ways of defining the term, in particular what I call the *legal, normative,* and *descriptive* definitions of it. I consider some of the problems with these definitions, including the fact that there are several competing candidates but no clear consensus on which is most appropriate. Nevertheless, I work through these problems in order to arrive at my own core definition of sexual harassment. These definitional issues could not practically be handled in sexual harassment training sessions, yet discussing them serves a goal shared with sexual harassment training, i.e., an enhanced understanding of the topic.

Second, the book takes its topic *seriously.* Sexual harassment is a pervasive problem that causes a range of serious harms to individuals, organizations, and society more broadly. One recent study of working women in the United States found that 58 per cent have been targets of behaviors that could be described as sexual harassment (Ilies et al.); for all industrialized nations, it is conservatively estimated that at least half of all women in the workplace have experienced sexual harassment (Sbraga and O'Donohue, 264). Each year, more than 10,000 charges of sexual harassment are filed with the U.S. Equal Employment Opportunity Commission.[1] Men are filing an increasing number of these charges: between 1990 and 2009, the proportion of charges of sexual harassment filed by men increased from 8 to 16 per cent.[2] Sexual harassment is also a problem in schools. A 2001 study by the American Association of University Women found that 81 per cent of high-school students have experienced some form of sexual harassment at least once during their school years. A survey conducted by the Association in 2011 of students in grades 7 to 12 found that 48 per cent were harassed during the previous year; 30 per cent encountered harassment through electronic means such as Facebook, e-mail, or texting (Hill and Kearl).[3] A survey of college students by the same organization in 2005 found that 62 per cent have experienced sexual harassment on their campuses (Hill and Silva).[4]

Victims of sexual harassment are harmed in a variety of ways. On college campuses, female victims are more likely to have difficulty studying and paying attention in class (Hill and Silva). Victims in the workplace typically report decreased job satisfaction, including disruption to, as well as dissatisfaction with, their relationships with co-workers, something that is otherwise a primary source of friendships for working people. Sexual harassment has deleterious effects on victims' mental health; they can suffer from anxiety, uncontrollable crying, anger, irritability, or depression. Psychological distress can also be expressed physically, such as in weight loss, dental and gastrointestinal problems, and fatigue. Some victims even experience symptoms of post-traumatic stress disorder (PTSD).[5]

Victims who quit their jobs to escape sexual harassment will suffer the financial hardship associated with doing so, but even if they remain in their jobs, their chances of advancing will be impeded by the sexual harassment they are experiencing. Reporting sexual harassment will also sometimes result in firing or other forms of retaliation (Sbraga and O'Donohue). Organizations in which sexual harassment is prevalent will suffer financial costs as well: victims of sexual harassment withdraw from their jobs; they miss work, neglect their duties, and in other ways their productivy decreases, as do their morale and their commitment to the organization.[6] Organizations also lose potentially good employees, both those within who are forced out or withdraw from their jobs because of sexual harassment, and prospective employees who do not apply because they know that either the organization or its industry is plagued by sexual harassment (Sbraga and O'Donohue).

Organizations also suffer legal costs due to sexual harassment.[7] In 1998, for example, Mitsubishi Motors settled for $34 million a sexual harassment lawsuit brought by hundreds of women workers at its auto plant in Normal, Illinois. The legal costs do not arise only in lawsuits; companies pay law firms and others to protect them from sexual harassment lawsuits, for example by running sexual harassment training for employees.[8]

Sexual harassment also harms individuals in ways that are less easy to quantify but are nevertheless severe. These are what we might call its *moral* harms, which are the subject of Chapter Two: "What Is Wrong with Sexual Harassment?" In this chapter, I examine normative definitions of sexual harassment, that is, definitions that specify what is morally wrong with it. That it is illegal is not what makes it wrong; it is wrong because it harms individuals in particular ways. In Chapter Two I identify these harms. I discuss first how sexual harassment is an attack on the *dignity* of its victims; it degrades and humiliates them, and it attacks their rights to autonomy and privacy. I then discuss how sexual harassment is also a tool of discrimination, principally wielded against women. It denies women the same opportunities to advance in the workplace or school as men. I examine how these views about the wrongness of sexual harassment often compete with each other. Those who write about the ethics of sexual harassment tend to favor one view about its wrongness over the other. I recommend a way to reconcile them and then identify a further harm caused by sexual harassment, one that has not received much attention. This harm is a consequence of the *at-will doctrine* that governs most employment in the United States. Because of this doctrine, as I explain, most workers do more work than is required of them in order to be compensated with promotion or continual employment. However, in workplaces in which there is sexual harassment, this extra work is not taken into account, so the worker is not compensated for it.

The third and final ideal that this book shares with my hypothetical sexual harassment training is that it aspires to be *useful*. It does so not only through the facts and other information it provides from the law and social sciences, but primarily by being a guide to thinking independently on the topic of sexual harassment. In this approach and through its choice of topics, the book's orientation is *philosophical*. In addition to drawing on the writings of philosophers on sexual harassment and related topics, I incorporate the approach of these thinkers by not merely presenting information about sexual harassment but by modeling and encouraging creative thinking about it;

readers are expected to use this approach to reach their own conclusions to the numerous questions raised by the topic.

For example, in Chapters Three and Four I introduce various questions about how and where sexual harassment can occur. In Chapter Three, "Where Can Sexual Harassment Occur?", I examine the contexts and circumstances in which sexual harassment can take place. While the book focuses mostly on sexual harassment in workplaces and schools, in this chapter I explore the conditions that allow for sexual harassment and whether they can be found in other contexts. For example, the chapter includes a lengthy discussion of how sexual harassment can occur within professional relationships, such as that between a lawyer and client, or a physician and patient. I closely examine one important condition for sexual harassment—power disparity—and discuss the nature of power and related concepts such as coercion. Also included is a discussion of *stranger harassment*, which involves behaviors that resemble sexual harassment but occur outside of workplaces, schools, or professional relationships. It occurs on public transportation, on the street, or in other public places. Most legal systems do not recognize it as a type of sexual harassment (and there are few laws that address it specifically). While the focus of the book is sexual harassment in workplaces and schools, I recognize that stranger harassment is a serious problem—one that is more pervasive than workplace harassment and can harm its victims in equally severe, although sometimes different, ways.[9]

In Chapter Four, "How Can Sexual Harassment Occur?", I continue the examination of power by looking at some of the behaviors that might cause sexual harassment. I focus particularly on how sexual harassment can occur within sexual or romantic relationships in which the partners hold positions of unequal power within an organization (most of the examples are of relationships of this sort within educational settings). In both Chapter Three and Four, as throughout the book, arguments are presented and some positions are defended, but these are meant primarily to provide readers with the resources to use in their own thinking on the issues.

This concern with usefulness culminates in the concluding chapter, "How Do We Prevent Sexual Harassment?" I draw on the main points raised in the earlier chapters to make specific recommendations about how individuals and organizations can prevent sexual harassment. In offering these recommendations, I explore in more depth some issues raised in previous chapters, such as whether sexual harassment laws should be expanded to cover stranger harassment. I also introduce some new issues. For example, I return to the present discussion about sexual harassment training and recommend changes for improving its delivery. Despite my complaints about my own experience with sexual harassment training and my worries about the usefulness of most such training, it could be an important tool in the fight against sexual harassment—if done correctly.

While the goals of understanding sexual harassment, appreciating its seriousness, and being useful should be the aspirations of any training in sexual harassment, this book goes beyond the typical training employees go through by looking at the topic in greater depth and equipping readers with the resources to do their own thinking on it. In these ways, the book should be more intellectually engaging than the typical sexual harassment training. It is hoped it is more interesting in other ways. Still, it shares the most important ostensible goal of sexual harassment training, which is to play some part in the prevention of sexual harassment.

At the end of each chapter are sets of review and discussion questions. The review questions are meant to test the reader's retention of the most important information provided in the chapter, while the discussion questions are designed to generate individual reflection or discussion within a group on the chapter's topics. Both sorts of questions could figure into classroom assignments. They are followed by suggestions for group activities. These are ways for collaboratively exploring the chapter's topics in more depth. They can be adapted and developed in various ways.

At the end of the book is a glossary of important terms. If a word is in the glossary, its first or most prominent appearance in the text is set in bold type. Following the glossary are three appendices. Appendix A provides some sample legal definitions of sexual harassment, including the ones that are most prominently discussed in the book. Appendix B is a list of websites relevant to sexual harassment. Some of these websites are referenced in the book; others provide further information and other resources on sexual harassment. Appendix C contains a list of films and television episodes that deal with sexual harassment, including brief descriptions of each. Some of these are probably not appropriate for classroom viewing (for example, *Pretty Persuasion* and *Secretary*), but may be viewed individually for insight (sometimes idiosyncratic) into sexual harassment.

NOTES

1   <http://www.eeoc.gov/eeoc/statistics/enforcement/sexual_harassment.cfm>; accessed 1 Dec. 2010.

2   Dave McGinn, "The new harassment: same-sex harassment in the workplace may be increasing—and it often takes the insidious form of humiliating comments and belittling abuse," *The Globe and Mail* [Toronto] 6 Oct. 2009: L1; see also Leonora Lapeter, "More Men Report Sexual Harassment by Other Men." *The St. Petersburg Times* 5 May 2007: 1B.

3   The reported cases of cyber-harassment consisted of receiving unwelcome sexual pictures or comments (20%), having sexual rumors spread about oneself (13%), or being called gay or lesbian in a negative way (12%). In all the categories except for the last one, women were more often the target of the cyber-harassment (e.g., 26 per cent of girls as opposed to 13 per cent of boys were victims of unwelcome sexual pictures or comments).

4   Male (61%) and female (62%) students are harassed almost equally, but the nature of the harassment is different (female students are the targets of sexual comments, gestures, looks, etc.; the harassment of male students more typically consists of their being called homophobic names), and women are more likely to experience sexual harassment that involves physical contact (35 per cent, as opposed to 29 per cent for males).

5   Sources and statistics for this and more information on the effects of workplace harassment can be found in Willness, Steel, and Lee, and in Sbraga and O'Donohue.

6   Again, see Willness, Steel, and Lee, and Sbraga and O'Donohue.

7   See Faley, Knapp, Kustis, and Dubois.

8   See Stuart Silverstein, "Fear of Lawsuits Spurs the Birth of New Industry," *Los Angeles Times* 27 June 1998: A1.

9   It is assumed that most readers have turned to this book for its coverage of the sexual harassment that tracks the majority of legal definitions, i.e., sexual harassment that occurs in workplaces and schools. That is a primary reason for the book's focus on this form of sexual harassment.

CHAPTER 1

What Is Sexual Harassment?

It is 1959. Sara, age 30, works on the assembly line at an auto-mobile factory in the United States.[1] She is the only woman working on her particular section of the line. She is friends with only a few of her co-workers, and almost none among those who work in her section. In fact, since she began her job most of her male co-workers have verbally ridiculed her for attempt-ing to do a "man's job," as they have put it. They have scrawled messages, mostly vulgar, expressing the same on her locker; they have hidden her tools, stolen her personal belongings, and once vandalized the one women's restroom in her section of the fac-tory, making it unusable for several days. Michael, who was once her only friend among her male co-workers, has not par-ticipated in these activities. However, a couple of months ago he communicated to Sara his romantic interest in her. She declined his invitation to go out on a date with him, but he has repeated his invitation. He has made it in person at the workplace, called her at home, and has slipped notes into her locker. His requests have become increasingly demanding, sexual, and in some cases hostile. She has asked him to stop, but he continues. Michael's actions have effectively ended their friendship; they have caused Sara to feel uncomfortable around him, and even at times fearful of her safety. The actions of Michael and her other co-workers have made the factory a very uncomfortable place for Sara to be. However, she needs her job and she is unlikely to find anything that pays as well and has the same benefits in her small town. So she continues working at the automobile factory.

Has Sara been sexually harassed? She has been the target, from several men, of physical and verbal actions that are unwelcome, offensive, and in some cases have caused her to fear for her safety. In order to decide whether any of these behaviors constitute sexual harassment, a helpful place to begin is with the origins and history of the term. Its origins are in the legal struggles in the United States in the 1970s against sexual harassment in the workplace, struggles that were very soon also directed against sexual harassment in schools. After reviewing this legal history, I will attempt to arrive at a definition of sexual harassment. Along the way, I discuss some of the problems with defining sexual harassment, including the fact that there are different *types* of definition. After reviewing these various definitions, I present what I call a *core* definition of sexual harassment that I will use throughout the book. It contains conditions shared by most other definitions of sexual harassment.

HISTORY AND PUBLIC AWARENESS OF SEXUAL HARASSMENT

Workplaces have always been sites of various forms of harassment, both sexual and non-sexual. The unequal power relationships within workplaces create an environment in which those with less power are susceptible to mistreatment by those with more power. Employees who also lack power outside the workplace are even more susceptible to harassment. While having a job improves their position within society, this has not always allowed them to escape the discrimination and other forms of harassment that they encounter in the rest of the world. They are vulnerable to harassment not only by their supervisors, but also by fellow employees who resent their presence in the workplace or who for other reasons perpetuate this mistreatment. Many of these employees have been women, and indeed women in the workplace have been the predominant victims of sexual forms of harassment.

In *The Sexual Harassment of Women in the Workplace, 1600 to 1993*, Kerry Segrave recounts the modern history of the mistreatment of women in the workplace. Among the many stories she tells, there is a very early one of a domestic servant in seventeenth-century England who was forced to submit to the sexual demands of her male employer when she was caught drinking his wine and threatened with being sent to prison (Segrave, 24). Being a domestic servant was once one of the few employment opportunities for women, who not only were frequently victims of abuse by the male heads of the household, but also had little recourse, legal or economic, for challenging this treatment. A widespread and persistent attitude toward domestic servants blamed them for their own abuse, attributing it to what was perceived as their inherently promiscuous natures, which welcomed or incited it. The most famous case in the United States of abuse of a domestic servant is that of Hester Vaughan, whose cause was taken up by the feminist newspaper started by Susan B. Anthony and Elizabeth Cady Stanton, *The Revoultion*. Vaughan immigrated to Pennsylvania from England and began working as a domestic servant. Her employer compelled her to have sex with him, and she eventually became pregnant. When her employer discovered this, he fired her. With no money and in ill health, she gave birth to the child alone in an unheated room. A few days later, she was discovered with her dead infant. In 1868, she was put on trial for infanticide, convicted, and sentenced to death. Through their advocacy on her behalf, *The Revolution* and the Working Women's Association were able to persuade the governor of Pennsylvania to pardon Vaughan (Segrave, 29–30).

For African-American women, jobs as domestic servants were among the most easily available after the Civil War. Most African Americans were excluded from the skilled professions;

African-American women were also excluded from factory jobs, leaving them dependent on jobs in the homes of their former white masters (Adams, 216). This left them vulnerable to the sexual exploitation that they suffered as slaves (Adams, 216–17). Under slavery, these women suffered "the extreme forms of sexual harassment—rape and concubinage" (Segrave, 17). As slaves, they had no power to resist this harassment, but even after the end of slavery, especially in the South, these forms of abuse did not end. Segrave quotes W.E.B. DuBois, who wrote in 1898 about many African Americans' view of domestic work: "Parents hate to expose ... their daughters to the ever-possible fate of concubinage" (Segrave, 34). The courts remained for a long time just as indifferent to their suffering as they were during slavery.

Jobs outside of the home, in factories or offices, offered women from all ethnic backgrounds little respite from sexual harassment. An inquiry in 1896 into working conditions at factories in Germany, for example, revealed various abuses of women, including verbal abuse, beatings, and rapes (Segrave, 43). Clerical workers were no less likely to be victims of sexual harassment. In a popular book of advice for working women published in 1935, the author tells her readers about the attentions that an attractive woman might receive from the men in the office, but she informs them that it is "quite harmless masculine attention that is not intended to be taken too seriously" (Segrave, 112).[2] She warns them that if this attention were ever taken too far, then the woman's only option would be to quit the job: "The one thing a girl absolutely cannot do is to carry troubles of this sort to anybody higher up. Unjust? Yes. But that is the way it is" (Segrave, 113). Employers were not willing to intervene; they did not consider it their responsibility and expected the women to handle these situations on their own. But even women who managed to join the "higher ups," or who pursued a profession with apparently more autonomy, did not escape sexual harassment (Segrave, 160–73).

Despite this history, the term "sexual harassment" did not come into widespread use until the 1970s.[3] Before then, various terms were used to describe the different actions that we now collectively refer to as sexual harassment, such as "sexual coercion," "sexual abuse," and "sexual exploitation."[4] Undoubtedly, the adoption of a single term to describe all of these behaviors has influenced our perception of them. We began to see them as connected, with similar causes and requiring similar remedies. It is a term that Sara would likely not have used to describe all the mistreatment she suffered; she would probably have used different terms to describe each of the different acts of harassment she experienced. With a single term, whose meaning encompasses most of those acts, she would have been more likely to see them as connected.

As I outline below, the term was adopted by lawyers fighting sexual harassment in the courts. As Catharine MacKinnon, an important legal scholar on sexual harassment, explains, the law has influenced public consciousness of sexual harassment: "Legitimized and sanctioned, the legal concept of sexual harassment reenters the society to participate in shaping the social definitions of what may be resisted or complained about, said aloud, or even felt" (MacKinnon, *Sexual Harassment*, 57). Studies have shown a correlation between the legal recognition of sexual harassment and public consciousness of it (see, for example, Uggen and Shinohara).

Perhaps more than the changes in the law that occurred in the 1970s and 1980s, several prominent stories about sexual harassment and public figures in the 1990s increased public awareness of sexual harassment in the United States. In 1991, Anita Hill testified at the U.S. Supreme Court confirmation hearings of Clarence Thomas. Hill, a lawyer, worked for Thomas at the Department of Education and the Equal Employment Opportunity Commission (EEOC). In her testimony, Hill alleged that Thomas initiated several sexually explicit conversations with her and pressured her to go out with him. She recounted the stress caused to her by these conversations and by Thomas's romantic overtures. Despite her allegations, Thomas's nomination to the Supreme Court was approved by the Senate. Then, the following year, U.S. Senator Bob Packwood was accused of sexual harassment by staffers and lobbyists. Many of the incidents, occuring over two decades, were recorded by Packwood in his diary, which was subpoenaed by the Senate Ethics Committee. The Committee voted unanimously to recommend his explusion from the Senate; he subsequently resigned.

In addition, allegations of sexual misconduct swirled around President Bill Clinton during most of his two terms in the 1990s. First, Paula Jones filed a lawsuit against Clinton alleging sexual harassment while he was governor of Arkansas. Her allegations were followed by others, including accusations of sexual assault, none of which was brought before a court. The Jones lawsuit was eventually settled out of court. Subsequently, in 1998, after denying it both publicly and in a deposition for the Jones lawsuit, Clinton admitted to having had sexual relations with White House intern Monica Lewinsky. His impeachment by the U.S. House of Representatives for perjury and obstruction of justice followed, but he was ultimately acquitted by the Senate.

As Christopher Uggen and Chika Shinohara report, the appearance of the term "sexual harassment" in the *The New York Times* peaked during the 1990s after very little mention in the 1980s (Uggen and Shinohara, 204–05), a trend we can reasonably assume was reflected in other media outlets. As the history in Segrave's book shows, this cannot be explained by an increase in incidents of sexual harassment. A better explanation is that the increased discussion of sexual harassment reflects, while also contributing to, an increase in public consciousness.

ORIGINS OF THE TERM

The term "sexual harassment" appeared in lawsuits in the 1970s that sought to grant relief to women suffering what was, in effect, sexual harassment under Title VII of the Civil Rights Act of 1964. There is no federal law in the United States that explicitly or directly prohibits sexual harassment in the workplace. Title VII prohibits discrimination in employment, and its most relevant part reads as follows:

It shall be an unlawful employment practice for an employer—
(1) to fail or refuse to hire or to discharge any individual, or otherwise to discriminate against any individual with respect to his compensation, terms, conditions, or privileges of employment, because of such individual's race, color, religion, sex, or national origin; or

(2) to limit, segregate, or classify his employees or applicants for
employment in any way which would deprive or tend to deprive
any individual of employment opportunities or otherwise adversely
affect his status as an employee, because of such individual's race,
color, religion, sex, or national origin.

The plaintiffs in these cases argued that sexual harassment was a
form of sex discrimination as described in Title VII. As I discuss further in Chapter Two, this strategy for combating sexual harassment
was not merely expedient; it reflected a particular philosophical and
legal understanding of the wrongness of sexual harassment. Such an
understanding of sexual harassment, as well as the legal strategy for
combating it, was developed and advocated by legal scholars such as
Catharine MacKinnon.[5]

MacKinnon and others argued that the actions that constitute
sexual harassment should be regarded by courts as discrimination
according to Title VII since, first, they were committed *because of*
the sex of the victims of these actions and, second, they deprived the
victims of employment opportunities. In a brief filed on behalf of the
plaintiffs in one of these cases, *Corne v. Bausch & Lomb, Inc.*, the
Equal Employment Opportunity Commission (which is responsible for
enforcing federal anti-discrimination laws) explains that sexual harassment is an "irrational impediment to job opportunities" because "the
choice between frequent unsolicited sexual advances and being unem-
ployed has a significant and clearly unwarranted effect on employment
opportunities."[6] In this case, the two female plaintiffs alleged that they
were forced to quit their jobs because of the sexual advances of their
boss. They argued that this was sex discrimination because they were
being denied employment benefits on the basis of their sex.

Initially the courts, including the one that heard the *Corne* suit, did
not accept the first part of the strategy, which was necessary for them
to find that sexual harassment was a type of discrimination prohibited by Title VII. In many cases, the courts concurred with a plaintiff's
view of the facts. Thus, they acknowledged that she had been deprived
of employment opportunities, but they refused to accept that this had

been done *because of* her sex. They tended to see sexual harassment as a "personal matter," and, while perhaps viewing it as immoral, they did not agree that it amounted to sex discrimination. Such a conclusion was reached by the court in *Barnes v. Train (Costle)* (1977), for example.[7] The plaintiff alleged that she had been fired after refusing the sexual advances of her supervisor. The court was convinced that this was the reason for her firing, but it concluded that this was different from being fired *because of* her sex. She was fired, instead, for her refusal to accept the sexual advances of her supervisor. While she was discriminated against, the basis of her discrimination was not prohibited by law; refusal to grant sexual favors to superiors is not a protected category in Title VII. It is not even implicitly protected by that statute, because both men and women are capable of refusing to grant sexual favors to supervisors. Therefore, it is not a characteristic possessed by one sex exclusively.

In 1976, however, a federal court did rule that sexual harassment is sex discrimination according to Title VII. This case, *Williams v. Saxbe*, involved a woman who was fired after refusing the sexual advances of her supervisor.[8] Although it was factually similar to the other cases, the court in this case concluded that the plaintiff would not have been subjected to such treatment *but for her sex*. One of the arguments of the defendant was that "sex discrimination may only be found when the policy or practice is applicable to only one of the genders because of the characteristics that are peculiar to one of the genders." The court rejected this argument. They concluded that in order for a practice to be discriminatory it does not need to be aimed at a characteristic specific to one gender: "That a rule, regulation, practice, or policy is applied on the basis of gender is alone sufficient for a finding of sex discrimination."

The view that sexual harassment is sex discrimination under Title VII was finally endorsed by the United States Supreme Court in 1986 in *Meritor Savings Bank v. Vinson*.[9] Mechelle Vinson had worked at Meritor Savings Bank for four years. She began as teller-trainee and rose in the ranks to assistant branch manager. In the fourth year of her employment she was fired for taking excessive sick leave. After her termination, Vinson sued the bank for sexual harassment. She alleged that her supervisor, Sidney Taylor, had coerced her to have sex with him at least 40 times, repeatedly demanded sexual favors from her, fondled her in front of the bank's other employees, and raped her on several occasions. The Court ruled that she had suffered discrimination according to Title VII. In its ruling, the court also endorsed some rulings by lower courts in earlier decisions, including that the defendant need not prove some tangible loss of benefit (such as her job) in order to claim sexual harassment. In doing so, the court adopted a distinction between two types of sexual harassment that had been drawn by lower courts, both forms of discrimination according to Title VII: *quid pro quo* and *hostile work environment*. The court ruled she had suffered the latter form of discrimination. I will explain each type of sexual harassment in the next section of this chapter.

The court also ruled that a company's lack of knowledge of sexual harassment does not automatically insulate it from liability, even if it has an anti-discrimination policy. The possible liability of employers extends to the actions of co-workers of a plaintiff, not just her supervisors. However, the court did not issue a definitive rule on employer liability because the case did not provide it with enough material for doing so. However, it did reject a standard of strict liability for employers; that is, the court ruled that employers were not automatically liable for the actions of their supervisors. In rulings on a pair of cases in 1998, the court revisited the issue of **vicarious liability**.[10] It ruled that employers are strictly liable for sexual harassment by their supervisors in cases that involve some tangible employment action, such as firing or demotion. In cases that involved a change in only the working conditions of the employee (see discussion of hostile work environments below), the employer can escape liability if it can prove that it acted to prevent harassment, such as by having a sexual harassment policy and complaint procedures and an employee who alleged sexual harassment failed to avail herself of these procedures.[11]

The court also ruled in *Meritor* that what matters in cases of sexual harassment is not whether the plaintiff *voluntarily* submitted to the harassment (for example, having sex with a supervisor in order to save her job); instead, what matters is whether the actions were "unwelcome." The court further decided that in determining whether actions were unwelcome, the behavior of the plaintiff, such as provocative speech or dress, is relevant.

Subsequent decisions by the U.S. Supreme Court and lower courts further developed the law surrounding sexual harassment, and they continue to do so. For example, in *Harris v. Forklift Systems, Inc.* (1993) the Supreme Court ruled that plaintiffs in sexual harassment suits do not need to prove that the sexual harassment caused them psychological harm or rendered them incapable of performing their job.[12] Sandra Day O'Connor, in her majority opinion, wrote that "Title VII comes into play before the harassing conduct leads to a nervous breakdown." We examine other court cases throughout this book.

In the United States, the **Equal Employment Opportunity Commission** is responsible for investigating complaints of discrimination in employment and, when it finds evidence supporting those complaints, filing lawsuits on behalf of the complainants.[13] Cases are heard before federal courts. Canada has a similar system, except a separate legal body considers the cases. The **Canadian Human Rights Commission** is charged with investigating complaints of discrimination according to the Canadian Human Rights Act, which was passed in 1977. Like the EEOC, it will attempt to resolve complaints through such methods as mediation, but if they are not successful, it can bring a case before the Canadian Human Rights Tribunal. The Tribunal hears cases only on discrimination, and all these cases are referred to it by the Canadian Human Rights Commission. The Canadian Human Rights Act covers only employees at federal agencies and departments, Crown corporations, and employers that fall under federal regulation such as banks, airlines, and television stations. Anti-harassment laws also exist at the provincial and territorial levels. Title VII is broader in application, but there are also anti-harassment laws at the state level.

In 1959, Sara had no such legal recourse against the harassment she suffered at her job. Her harassment occurred not only before courts recognized sexual harassment as a form of discrimination in the United States, but also before passage of the anti-discrimination legislation of Title VII. She could have brought civil suits for some of the harassment she suffered, but only for recognized torts, such as assault, destruction of property, or emotional distress. It was only Title VII and the courts' application of it to sexual harassment that allowed women to sue for discrimination and for the much larger and more various kinds of behaviors that can constitute it.

Sara would have been in the same situation if she had experienced this harassment as a student in an educational setting. Title IX of the 1972 Education Act Amendments prohibits discrimination in educational institutions that receive federal funds. In 1977, several students sued Yale University over sexual harassment. The plaintiffs in the case (*Alexander v. Yale*) were five female students and a male faculty member.[14] Some of them claimed to be the direct victims of sexual harassment; others, including the male faculty member, alleged that incidents of sexual harassment on the Yale campus impeded them in their efforts to do their jobs, whether learning or teaching (Simon; Baker, 58–62).[15] Only the case of one of these students made it to trial, and it was later dismissed after she graduated from Yale. Nevertheless, the court ruled in the case that sexual harassment counts as sex discrimination under Title IX. A 1992 Supreme Court decision, *Franklin v. Gwinnett County Public Schools*, affirmed that students who have been sexually harassed by school employees can sue for monetary damages (sexual harassment in schools is the focus of Chapter Four).[16]

In addition to schools and workplaces, there are laws governing sexual harassment in the military. There are also professional codes for lawyers, physicians, and others that prohibit sexual harassment and actions that could lead to sexual harassment; these are discussed in Chapter Three. But in the United States there are no laws prohibiting harassment outside of these institutions. Let us expand Sara's story briefly in order to illustrate this:

On top of the discomfort Sara feels at work, her only social hangout in her small town has become a place that Sara no longer enjoys visiting. When she goes by herself or with friends, she is constantly ogled by the male patrons, verbally propositioned by them, often with vulgar language, and has other sexual or obscene comments directed at her. On more than one occasion she has been touched inappropriately by one of the male patrons. Her protestations against this behavior have made no difference, so she has decided to stop visiting the bar. She is left with very few enjoyable social interactions in her life.

Her experiences in the bar are similar to those at her workplace; she is being singled out for this demeaning treatment because of her gender. Anyone experiencing this treatment today in a business or school in the United States would be considered a victim of sexual harassment according to the law. But outside of such contexts, the identical actions would not be regarded by courts as sexual harassment. We will eventually examine a law from Israel that would consider Sara's treatment in the bar as sexual harassment, and we will consider whether definitions other than legal ones should also cover cases like this.

DEFINING THE TERM

While courts in the United States and elsewhere have decided numerous sexual harassment cases, a stable, coherent definition of sexual harassment is still elusive. As the philosopher Elizabeth Anderson laments, "Sexual harassment is not a unified phenomenon, either normatively or sociologically" (Anderson, 285). Anderson and others point out that while the law has influenced our extra-legal understanding of sexual harassment, it has also to some extent confused it. For example, we will see how courts have applied the term to actions that are not typically considered sexual harassment, and have failed to apply it to those that most of us would consider sexual harassment. So, for this and other reasons, the law cannot be our only guide in defining sexual harassment. In this section, we try to work through some of the problems of defining sexual harassment in order to arrive at a core definition that we can work with and refine through the rest of this book.

The most desirable sort of definition is one that provides the *necessary* and *sufficient* conditions for the application of a term. That is, it will specify everything that *must* be the case for the term to be correctly applied (necessary conditions) and all those things whose truth is *enough* for the term to be correctly applied (sufficient conditions). The set of all necessary conditions is typically *conjointly* sufficient for the correct application of the term. For example, the presence of oxygen is among the necessary conditions for water (H_2O). The other necessary conditions are the other molecules of which it is comprised and their number; the set of all these necessary conditions *jointly* provides the sufficient conditions for something being water. So, for water you need oxygen, but oxygen is not enough; you also need hydrogen.

For a definition of sexual harassment, a set of necessary and sufficient conditions would state all those actions that must be present in cases of sexual harassment (necessary conditions), and those behaviors or actions whose presence is enough for there to be sexual harassment (sufficient conditions). Specifying actions will probably not be enough, because the very same actions could be sexual harassment in one context but not sexual harassment in another. Therefore, we will also need to pay attention to where those actions occur and somehow incorporate that into our definition.

If we could provide necessary and sufficient conditions for sexual harassment, then we would acquire much needed insight into its nature. However, at least one philosopher, Margaret Crouch, has concluded that such a definition is not possible. She suggests that sexual harassment resists definition in terms of necessary and sufficient conditions, instead considering it to be a **family resemblance concept** (Crouch, 5). The influential twentieth-century philosopher Ludwig Wittgenstein introduced the notion of a family resemblance concept (Wittgenstein, §66ff), his most famous example being *game*. This is a familiar concept to all of us and one that we can easily apply in most cases. When we have complete information about an activity, that is, when we know what is being done and why, we are usually able to say whether or not it is a game. However, among all the things we call games, there does not seem to be a single characteristic, nor even a set of them, that each possesses. Some games are played with balls, others with game pieces; some are played on fields, others on boards; and while many are performed for fun, professional athletes often seem not to be having fun while playing their games. While most games are played according to explicit rules, some are not (for example, a child throwing a ball against a wall). Even if we did not count those as games, being governed by rules could not be a sufficient condition for games since there are many activities that are governed by rules but are not games (faculty meetings, dancing, etiquette, and so on).

Wittgenstein called concepts such as *game* family resemblance concepts because the relationship between their referents resembles that between the physical characteristics of family members. Think of a family photo of parents and their children. If you examine the physical appearance of each family member, you will typically not be able to detect one characteristic, let alone a set of them, that *every* family member possesses. Instead, some—but not all—will have the same nose, some the same hair color; some will be similar in height or weight; and so on. If sexual harassment were a family resemblance concept, then among the various actions we are willing to label as sexual harassment, there will not be some single characteristic or set of them that they all possess. In defining the term, the best we could do would be to give representative examples, and if we needed to decide whether a certain behavior was sexual harassment, our decision would be based on how closely it resembled these examples.

Yet the term sexual harassment, by its very construction, seems to suggest a shared characteristic: it is harassment that is *sexual* in nature. So any act of harassment that has the characteristic of being sexual is sexual harassment. Assuming there is little difficulty in defining the component terms, it seems a straightforward matter to pick out cases of sexual harassment. However, this seeming simplicity of the term has actually been the source of some confusion. The confusion is a consequence of the ambiguity of the term "sexual."

U.S. courts have recognized sexual harassment even when there is no sexual content to the harassment. In one of these cases (*Hall v. Gus Construction Co.*), three women who worked as traffic controllers (or "flag persons") for a road construction company sued their employer for sexual harassment.[17] They were the only women on their crew, and they suffered various sorts of abuse from their male co-workers. While some of the abuse was sexual in nature (for example, being subject to sexual propositions), others were not. For example, a male co-worker urinated in the water bottle of one woman; several men urinated into the gas tank of one of the women's car, causing damage to the car. A truck used by the women had a carbon monoxide leak that would cause the driver to become drowsy. The women's requests to have the car repaired were ignored, forcing them to take turns driving the truck for brief periods. The defendants argued that since these acts had no sexual content, they should not be considered in a sexual harassment lawsuit. The court disagreed and concluded that any unequal treatment that would not occur "but for the sex" of the victim is sexual harassment. To count as sexual harassment, the court ruled, the harassment does not need to be a sexual advance or have any sexual overtones.

The harassment Sara endures from most of her male co-workers is sexual insofar as it refers to, and is because of, her sex, but it is not sexual in content. That is, it consists of insults and other abuses that refer to her sex and is motivated by an antipathy toward her sex, but it does not refer to sexual acts. The harassment of Sara by Michael, her former friend at the factory, however, *is* sexual. It is motivated by a sexual desire for her and consists of acts that do have sexual content. If her case were heard in a U.S. court today, both sets of behavior would likely be regarded as sexual harassment.

The courts' willingness to call both forms of harassment sexual can be explained by the ambiguity of the word "sexual." It can refer to either sexual activities or biological sex. The latter is often used synonymously with gender.[18] Since all of the harassment Sara endures is because she is a woman, courts are willing to classify it all as sexual harassment. But does this conform to our ordinary understanding of sexual harassment? It seems not. In the first lawsuits that used the term sexual harassment, the term referred to behavior with sexual content. It also seems that we typically use the term today to refer to behaviors that are in some way sexual, in the sense of sexual activity. Since the courts understand sexual harassment to be a kind of discrimination, they tend to conflate it with all forms of gender discrimination. However, what Sara experiences from her co-workers and what the women at Gus Construction experienced is *gender* harassment. While sexual harassment might be a type of gender harassment (we will explore this further in Chapter Two), the two are nevertheless distinct.

Courts have conflated gender and sexual harassment in cases of hostile environment sexual harassment. This is one of the two types of sexual harassment that the Supreme Court distinguished in *Meritor Savings Bank v. Vinson*. The other sort of sexual harassment, **quid pro quo**, is inescapably sexual. "Quid pro quo" is a Latin phrase that means "something for something." It occurs when employment benefits are conditioned on the fulfillment of sexual demands. An example would be a supervisor threatening to fire an employee unless she has sex with him. Other sorts of employment benefits could be denied to the employee for failing to comply with a sexual demand, such as promotions, raises, or work assignments. For quid pro quo harassment to occur, the harasser must have some authority over the victim, specifically the power to confer or withhold employment benefits. But even when the perpetrator of the harassment does not have such authority, the victim might still have a case under Title VII.

Hostile environment sexual harassment refers to a practice and not a particular act. It occurs when one sex is selected for disparate treatment in a way that, as the EEOC guidelines put it, is "intimidating, hostile, or offensive" or interferes with the employee's work. This form of harassment can be committed by co-workers and supervisors. It can consist of verbal conduct, such as offensive language, demeaning or insulting comments, requests for sexual favors made by co-workers, and so on. The display of pornographic pictures, sexually themed cartoons or graffiti, and other offensive visual material can also create a hostile work environment, as can physical conduct, such as unwelcome touching. Other forms of disparate treatment can constitute a hostile work environment, such as less desirable work assignments, greater scrutiny of work performance, or being overly criticized or in other ways demeaned in front of co-workers. The conduct need not lead to the loss of a tangible job benefit, such as a raise or promotion. The harm consists of being compelled to work in an environment that is, in any of these various ways, hostile. In another contrast with quid pro quo cases, more than one offensive act is required for there to exist a hostile work environment. The conduct needs to be frequent and pervasive. Finally, as we discussed, according to U.S. law the conduct does not have to be sexual in nature, in the sense of referring to sexual activity or behavior.

This brings us back to our problem of defining sexual harassment. How we should define it depends ultimately on our reasons for seeking a definition. If we want to know what actions the law considers to be sexual harassment, then we want a *legal* definition. This can be found in legislation, court decisions, or government regulations. It will specify what actions are illegal. In the United States, the governing definition in federal law of sexual harassment is provided by the EEOC in its *Guidelines on Discrimination Because of Sex: Sexual Harassment*. Courts are guided by it in making their decisions, and employers refer to it in crafting their anti-harassment policies:

> Unwelcome sexual advances, requests for sexual favors, and other verbal or physical conduct of a sexual nature constitute sexual harassment when (1) submission to such conduct is made either explicitly or implicitly a term or condition of an individual's employment, (2) submission to or rejection of such conduct by an individual is used as the basis for employment decisions affecting such individual, or (3) such conduct has the purpose or effect of unreasonably interfering with an individual's work performance or creating an intimidating, hostile, or offensive working environment.[19]

This definition covers both the quid pro quo and hostile environment types of sexual harassment.

Definitions in other legal systems will differ not only in wording, but also in scope and application. For example, French law does not recognize the hostile work environment type of sexual harassment (Saguy, 607). The Canada Labour Code definition of sexual harassment restricts it to actions that have sexual content. It defines sexual harassment as "any conduct, comment, gesture or contact of a sexual nature (*a*) that is likely to cause offence or humiliation to any employee; or (*b*) that might, on reasonable grounds, be perceived by that employee as placing a condition of a sexual nature on employment or on any opportunity for training or promotion" (Part III, Division XV.1). International and regional organizations such as the United Nations and the European Union also have definitions of sexual harassment. Examples of these definitions are reproduced in Appendix A.

We look for a legal definition of sexual harassment when we want to know how courts and other organs of a legal system understand sexual harassment. We would consult such a definition if we were developing an anti-harassment policy for a school or a business, if we were a lawyer advising a client, or if we were trying to determine whether there is any legal remedy for the harassment we were experiencing at work. However, there are other reasons for asking for a definition of sexual harassment. For example, we could be interested in what makes sexual harassment *morally wrong*. There are definitions whose conditions allow us to identify actions that are sexual harassment and that imply that all actions meeting those conditions are immoral (the conditions also partly explain why those actions are immoral). A definition of this sort might be different from any legal definition. While laws ideally prohibit immoral actions, they typically do not prohibit *every* immoral action. So the scope of this sort of definition might be broader than a legal definition. It could also be narrower relative to some legal definition if the legal definition proscribes actions that are not immoral.[20] Therefore, not everything that is sexual harassment according to this sort of definition will be illegal, but it will be immoral. We might want such a definition simply to improve our understanding of what is wrong with sexual harassment, or we might want to know whether some behavior we have witnessed is immoral. This definition could also be important when advocating for legislation on sexual harassment.

Finally, we might be interested in sexual harassment as a social phenomenon. This is the sort of definition that sociologist or psychologists would use in their research, and it would be neutral as to the illegality or immorality of the actions it considers to be sexual harassment. This kind of definition is determined mostly by our everyday understanding of sexual harassment—that is, how the term is commonly used outside of courts or ethics textbooks.

Let us call these three possible definitions, respectively, the *legal*, *normative*, and *descriptive* definitions of sexual harassment. There will be a legal definition of sexual harassment for every legal system that has laws pertaining to sexual harassment. These will include federal and local laws, as well as the definitions crafted by certain international and regional organizations. There *should* be just one normative definition of sexual harassment, but we will examine several competing candidates for this definition in the next chapter. There could also be various contenders for the descriptive definition of sexual harassment, but several of them might be equally correct. How the term is used might vary from country to country, or region to region, as well as across time periods. It might also vary across genders and ages. Therefore, a single, uniform descriptive definition of sexual harassment is probably elusive, but there still should be a great deal of similarity between descriptive definitions.

Given the various ways of defining sexual harassment, Margaret Crouch's contention that sexual harassment is a family resemblance concept might seem plausible. It is at least a good way to characterize the relationship among all of these definitions. However, each definition attempts to specify necessary and sufficient conditions for sexual harassment. This is a practical requirement of the legal definitions, since a legal definition that is incapable of clearly saying of any action whether or not it is sexual harassment is not a very useful one. A definition based in necessary and sufficient conditions does that the best; however, as we have seen, in the United States the legal definition of sexual harassment is constantly evolving, and there remains a lack of consensus among jurists, legislators, and others as to what these necessary and sufficient conditions are. Those who propose normative definitions also attempt to construct definitions that specify necessary and sufficient conditions, but as I discuss in the next chapter, the issue of constructing a correct normative definition is even more contentious.

A descriptive definition will reflect our ordinary use of the term, but we should not expect that to conform to the strictures of a definition grounded in necessary and sufficient conditions. In fact, Wittgenstein's purpose in introducing the notion of a family resemblance concept was to disabuse us of the assumption that all the concepts of natural language could be defined in terms of necessary and sufficient conditions. Language arose and continues to evolve in ways that do not make that a reasonable assumption, and it seems that Crouch's primary reason for thinking that "sexual harassment" is a family resemblance concept is her rejection of this assumption. If it should be rejected, then our descriptive definitions should not aspire to provide necessary and sufficient conditions for the application of the term sexual harassment. We may still strive to provide these conditions in our legal and normative definitions, but such definitions must be related to the ordinary use of the term. If a definition based in necessary and sufficient conditions does not allow that, then we should abandon it for one that is closer to the common and everyday understanding of the term.

Despite these issues, it should be possible to isolate elements that most definitions share. Legal, normative, and descriptive definitions of sexual harassment typically include at least three conditions sufficient for an action to be considered sexual harassment:

1) the action is unwelcome;
2) it is of a sexual nature; and
3) the person or persons responsible for the action has power over the person who is the target of the actions.

As for the first condition, sexual harassment is always unwelcomed by its target. Definitions will vary in how they determine whether the actions were unwelcomed. For example, U.S. law holds that voluntarily submitting to the actions—for example, submitting to a quid pro quo demand—is no indication of whether the behavior was welcomed. U.S. law does allow consideration of the alleged victim's behavior, such as dress and language, in determining whether a behavior was welcomed; in the next chapter, we will consider some normative definitions whose standards for unwelcomeness do not even include explicit objections to the actions by the victim. The second condition captures the original and common understanding of sexual harassment. The sexual content of the harassment distinguishes it from other types of harassment, including other types of gender harassment more broadly. The third condition is how we account for the *context* of the actions that fall under 1) and 2). Only unwelcome actions of a sexual nature that are performed in the context of an imbalance of power count as sexual harassment. However, in Chapter Three I discuss a legal definition that does not require there to be a difference in power between the harasser and the victim. The third condition is worded to cover hostile work environments. In such cases, the harasser need not have any power over the victim. It suffices that the harasser act in a context in which some liable person (for example, an employer) does hold power over the victim.

Whether these conditions are necessary varies from definition to definition. For example, we have seen that according to U.S. law it is not necessary that the action be sexual in nature. U.S. courts use the "but for the sex" criteria in identifying cases of a sexual nature; i.e., the action would not have been performed if its target had been the other sex. This condition is satisfied most clearly when the action is sexual in nature, but as long as the victim is harassed because of her sex, then the harassment counts as sexual harassment according to U.S. law. Other legal definitions, such as that contained in the Canada Labour Code, can restrict sexual harassment to actions that have sexual content.

These three conditions are jointly sufficient for sexual harassment. That is, whenever all three occur, there is a case of sexual harassment. These conditions are found in almost all of the definitions of sexual harassment that we will examine in this book. Let us call them the *core* definition of sexual harassment. We will make use of this definition in various ways—including refining it—throughout the book.

APPLYING THE TERM

Let us now consider Sara's case again, with reference to the three types of definition. First, according to the legal definition, Sara is not sexually harassed. The harassment occurs in the United States in 1959, which is before both the passage of Title VII in 1964 and the courts' recognition in the 1970s and 1980s that it covers sexual harassment. While her case might fit today's legal definition of sexual harassment, when it occurred there was no such legal definition. Second, according to some normative definitions, some of the actions against her could be sexual harassment. The actions did not become immoral only when they became illegal; indeed, their immorality, in part, motivated the recognition that they should be illegal. Finally, whether Sara is sexually harassed according to a descriptive definition depends on which descriptive definition we consult. When the harassment occurred, the term "sexual harassment" was not widely used, but according to most descriptive definitions today, Sara is sexually harassed.

There is also the issue of which of the actions against her can be considered sexual harassment. According to the U.S. legal definition, the actions by her co-workers would—if they occurred today—be considered sexual harassment, but they fall outside the scope of our core definition and most normative and descriptive definitions because they are not of a sexual nature, i.e., not related directly to sexual behavior. Since they are directed at her because of her "gender" (i.e., her biological sex), they can still be considered *gender* harassment. The actions of Michael would be considered sexual harassment by most definitions, since they involve direct reference to sexual behavior. Those of the patrons at the bar, however, even though many are explicitly sexual in nature, would not be considered sexual harassment by most legal definitions because they occur outside of the areas covered by most sexual harassment laws, i.e., workplaces and schools. A focus of Chapter Three will be whether actions such as these can still be considered sexual harassment either normatively or descriptively.

SUMMARY

Our topic in this chapter has been the definition of sexual harassment. We began by exploring how the meaning of sexual harassment developed in the law, mostly United States law. We then recognized that there are other sorts of definition for sexual harassment; in addition to legal definitions, there are normative and descriptive ones. After considering the goals of, and problems with, defining sexual harassment, we arrived at a core definition of sexual harassment that contains conditions shared by most candidates for all three sorts of definition. It states that actions count as sexual harassment when 1) they are unwelcome, 2) they are of a sexual nature, and 3) the person (or persons) responsible for the actions has power over the person who is the target of the actions.

REVIEW QUESTIONS

1. In what decade did "sexual harassment" become a legal term of art and sexual harassment was first recognized by U.S. Courts as discrimination according to Title VII? What are some of the cases heard by the courts? When did the U.S. Supreme Court recognize sexual harassment as a violation of Title VII of the Civil Rights Act of 1964?
2. What are the responsibilities of the Equal Employment Opportunity Commission and the Canadian Human Rights Commission?
3. What is a definition based in necessary and sufficient conditions? What is a family resemblance concept?
4. What are the two types of sexual harassment?

5. What are some differences between legal, normative, and descriptive definitions of sexual harassment?

DISCUSSION QUESTIONS

1. Should U.S. Courts more clearly distinguish between sexual harassment and what they consider to be other types of "gender harassment"? Instead of treating it as a kind of discrimination, should there be a separate law devoted to sexual harassment?

2. Some victims of sexual harassment—e.g., African-American women, gays and lesbians, and so on—are also victims of other forms of discrimination. What factors might make them more susceptible to sexual harassment?

3. Some might say that Sara was not sexually harassed, given that there was no law against sexual harassment, or even a legal definition of it, when the actions directed against her occurred. Do you agree? Why or why not?

4. Is sexual harassment a family resemblance concept? If not, what should be some of its necessary and sufficient conditions?

GROUP ACTIVITY

Working together in a large group, create a list of offensive behaviors in the workplace or classroom. Discuss which are sexual harassment, which are discriminatory, and which should be prohibited by a) law, b) morality, and c) professional codes of ethics (these categories are not mutually exclusive).

NOTES

1 This vignette and those that begin the other chapters are fictional. They are inspired by case law and other reported examples of actual sexual harassment.

2 The book Segrave discusses and quotes from is Francis Maule, *She Strives to Conquer* (New York: Funk & Wagnalls, 1935).

3 Some scholars claim that the term was "coined" in the 1970s (Sterba, 231; Crouch, 3). This is difficult to prove, but what is true is that the term "sexual harassment" did not become a *term of art* until the 1970s; that is, it was deliberately adopted by people involved in the law to refer to a kind of workplace harassment that had been variously described until then

(MacKinnon, *Sexual Harassment*, 250n13; Baker, 31; Crouch, 3). This section of the chapter reviews some of this legal history.

4 The term "sexual harassment" has since been adopted by other languages, for example, *harcèlement sexuel* in French and *seku hara* in Japanese.

5 MacKinnon's seminal 1979 book on sexual harassment, from which I quote extensively in the next chapter, is titled *Sexual Harassment of Working Women*.

6 Quoted in Baker, 19; Brief of the Equal Employment Opportunity Commission as Amicus Curiae in Opposition to Defendants' Motions to Dismiss, Dated 17 January 1975, *Corne v. Bausch and Lomb*, 390 F. Supp. 161.

7 *Barnes v. Costle*, 561 F.2d 983 (D.C. Cir. 1977).

8 *Williams v. Saxbe*, 413 F. Supp. 654 (D.D.C. 1976).

9 *Meritor Savings Bank v. Vinson*, 477 U.S. 57 (1986).

10 *Burlington Industries, Inc. v. Ellerth*, 524 U.S. 742 (1998) and *Faragher v. City of Boca Raton*, 524 U.S. 775 (1998).

11 See Oppenheimer, and EEOC's "Enforcement Guidance on Vicarious Employer Liability for Unlawful Harassment by Supervisors," at <http://www.eeoc.gov/policy/docs/harassment.html>; accessed September 11, 2010.

12 *Harris v. Forklift Systems, Inc.*, 510 U.S. 17 (1993).

13 In addition to Title VII of the Civil Rights Act of 1964, the Commission enforces the Equal Pay Act of 1963, the Age Discrimination in Employment Act of 1967, Title I of the Americans with Disabilities Act of 1990, and the Genetic Information Nondiscrimination Act of 2008.

14 *Alexander v. Yale University*, 459 F. Supp. I (D. Conn. 1977), affirmed 631 F. 2d 178 (2nd Cir. 1980).

15 For example, one of the students, Ronnie Alexander, claimed that her flute teacher forced her to have sex with him, and since Yale had in place no procedures for her to complain, she felt compelled to change her course of study, abandoning both music and the flute. The male faculty member, John Winkler, claimed that incidents of sexual harassment had created mistrust of male professors, making it difficult for him to do his job.

16 *Franklin v. Gwinnett County Public Schools*, 503 U.S. 60 (1992)

17 *Hall v. Gus Construction Co.*, 842 F.2d 1010 (8th Cir. 1988).

18 While in this book I will follow the courts and often use "sex" and "gender" interchangeably, the two terms can be used to refer to two importantly different concepts (see, for example, MacKinnon, *Sexual Harassment*, 150–51). The former refers to a biological distinction, whereas the latter refers to a cultural one. As cultural, gender is a category that is malleable and not necessarily connected to biological sex. It represents culturally mandated expectations on how men and women are supposed to look and behave. In the next chapter, I will discuss how gender stereotypes, and what is known as gender-policing, enforce these expectations.

19 Code of Federal Regulations: Title 29, Sec. 1604.11

20 Many have argued that the U.S. legal definition is too broad. However, the most influential of these arguments contend that the definition prohibits actions that the law should not, not that these actions are moral.

CHAPTER 2

What Is Wrong with Sexual Harassment?

Roger works in a large office with many employees, almost equally made up of men and women. The employees' desks are arranged in pairs across an open room. The supervisor's office is a small glass cubicle located in one corner of the room. The desk across from Roger's is occupied by Charlie. Although Roger and Charlie are not friends outside of work, they converse with each other throughout the workday. They discuss their wives and children, sports, and their hobbies. Charlie's hobby is taxidermy. He likes to tell Roger about his latest taxidermy project. This typically involves his describing in detail the process of preparing the animal for mounting. Roger does not share this interest in taxidermy. In fact, he is a vegetarian and a donor to several animal rights organizations, and he finds Charlie's detailed descriptions of his taxidermy projects disgusting. He has told this to Charlie on many occasions and while doing so will cause Charlie to change the topic, he eventually returns to it. Roger has not complained to their supervisor about Charlie's conversations because he does not want to get Charlie into trouble.

Their supervisor, Jennifer, does not mind that her employees have personal conversations with each other. In fact, Jennifer passes through the office several times a day and holds conversations with employees at their desks. Jennifer's favorite topic of conversation is sex. She discusses her sexual interests, fantasies, and experiences. In addition to these conversations, which she has with employees of both sexes, Jennifer frequently e-mails her employees "dirty jokes" and links to pornographic websites. Most employees, including Roger, are offended by Jennifer's conversations and e-mails. Roger has asked her to refrain from them several times, but he has taken no other action. Only a few other employees offended by Jennifer's behavior have objected to her personally; no one has reported her.

According to what we learned in Chapter One, it seems that Jennifer has created a hostile work environment.[1] The reluctance of Roger and the other employees to challenge her behavior either directly or by reporting it is not unusual for people in their positions; neither is their reluctance to quit their jobs over it (Lundberg-Love and Marmion, 87–88; Gruber, 51–53). Employees can feel that reporting sexual harassment will only make the situation worse, cause them to be labeled a trouble-maker, hurt their chances of advancing in the company, or make them a target of retaliation (Gruber, 53; Lundberg-Love and Marmion, 88). Leaving a job over sexual harassment is not a better option for many employees. It requires them to find a new job, which is typically not easy, and it can force them to give up seniority or other benefits at their current job. If they quit before finding a new job, then—in places like the United States—they risk losing their health insurance. There are also some less tangible attachments a worker has to his or her job. For example, since many workers spend much of their time at their workplaces, their job becomes their primary arena for social interaction. They form and cultivate friendships at their jobs, so leaving a job often means an end to those relationships. One's job is also an important part of one's identity, which can be forced to undergo alteration when quitting a job.

These are some of the reasons why people who have supervisors like Jennifer decide to do nothing except, to the best of their ability, ignore the behavior. Perhaps Roger takes no action because he believes that there is simply nothing he could do that would remedy the situation at his workplace, other than leaving it. Roger is being harassed by his supervisor, but his supervisor is what is often described as an "**equal-opportunity harasser**." As we learned in Chapter One, federal sexual harassment law in the United States is based on anti-discrimination law, in particular, Title VII of the Civil Rights Act of 1964. This law prohibits discrimination in employment on the basis of gender, ethnicity, religion, or national origin. As we also learned, courts eventually recognized sexual harassment as a form of gender discrimination. Jennifer, however, does not discriminate on the basis of gender. She subjects both the men and the women in her office to her sexual communications.

In 1998, the Supreme Court unanimously ruled in *Oncale v. Sundowner Offshore Services, Inc.* that sexual harassment had occurred in a case in which both the plantiff and the perpetrators of the sexual harassment were male.[2] Joseph Oncale was an offshore oil-rig worker who quit his job after repeated harassment by his male supervisor and co-workers. The harassment included "sex-related, humiliating actions," a sexual assault, and a threat of rape. He sued for both hostile work environment and quid pro quo harassment. The court's ruling established that men could be victims of sexual harassment; it also established that sexual harassment can occur when the harasser and the victim are of the same sex (so-called **same-sex sexual harassment**). Equally important, the court stated that the harassment does not need to be motivated by sexual desire for the victim by the harasser; it can occur when the harassing behavior expresses hostility toward the victim because of his or her sex. But even when there is a sexual content to the behavior, as there sometimes is in "male-on-male horseplay" and other forms of "ordinary socializing," such behavior is not sexual harassment unless it constitutes "discrimination because of sex." That is, it has to be inferred that the victim would not be a target of the behavior if he or she were of a different sex.

However, the requirement that the behavior be discriminatory creates what many see as a loophole in the federal law on sexual harassment: whenever both sexes are being harassed, the harasser is not guilty of sexual harassment. In 2000, an appeals court ruled against a married couple that brought a suit of sexual harassment against their supervisor (*Holman v. Indiana*).[3] The couple claimed that the supervisor sexually harassed *both* of them, but rather than making the case more severe, the harasser's equitable treatment of husband and wife actually made him immune to charges of sexual harassment. As the court explained: "Title VII does not cover the 'equal opportunity' or 'bisexual' harasser ... because such a person is not discriminating on the basis of sex. He is not treating one sex better (or worse) than the other; he is treating both sexes the same (albeit badly)." The court recognized that there might be some policy concerns about allowing "equal opportunity" harassers to fall outside the scope of sexual harassment law, but as they point out, "It is not the province of federal courts to expand the language of a statute that is clearly limited."[4]

Consequently, neither Roger nor the other employees who are subjected to Jennifer's behavior would be likely to succeed in their legal actions. There might be some remedies specific to their company of which they can avail themselves, but they cannot use federal law to remedy their situation.[5] But even if the courts do not think so, is there not still something wrong with Jennifer's behavior? In this chapter, we set the legal issues mostly to the side and look at the issue of the wrongness of sexual harassment from a moral perspective. If we believe that an equal-opportunity harasser's behavior is wrong, then it appears that we need to identify something wrong with it other than discrimination. In the next section, I examine views about the wrongness of sexual harassment that attempt to explain what is wrong with Jennifer's treatment of Roger and the other employees in the office. After discussing some problems with these views, I return to the view that the wrongness of sexual harassment is discrimination, considering different versions of this approach and their problems. The chapter concludes by suggesting how to resolve the problems with these competing views and identifying a further wrong with sexual harassment that none of these views addresses.

My focus in this chapter is on hostile work environments. That is, most of the examples and discussion revolve around this type of sexual harassment. In subsequent chapters, I focus on the quid pro quo kind of sexual harassment, although much of the discussion in this chapter also has application to quid pro quo cases.

SEXUAL HARASSMENT AS WRONGFUL COMMUNICATION

According to the philosopher Edmund Wall, sexual harassment is morally wrong because it violates the victim's privacy and autonomy rights. It does this, according to Wall, by being a case of what he calls *wrongful communication*. The rights that Wall believes such communication violates are *moral* rights. While some rights of this sort might be enforced by the law, legal rights and moral rights are nevertheless distinct. For example, a moral right can be violated even when there are no laws to protect it, whereas legal rights are only established by law.[6] It is both immoral and illegal to steal from someone, for instance; however, if you take someone into your confidence and share personal information with her, and she then shares that information with another person without your permission, she has violated your privacy rights—she has done something immoral, but not necessarily anything illegal.

What establishes our moral rights is a complex affair.[7] There are moral skeptics and nihilists who, respectively, doubt or deny that we have such rights. The branch of ethics known as *ethical theory* is concerned with identifying and justifying these rights. This book is partly a work in *applied ethics*, in which one assumes certain moral rights and then applies them in an effort to resolve specific moral dilemmas. That is how we will proceed: we will assume that people possess a range of widely recognized rights, including rights to privacy and autonomy. The questions that will concern us involve the extent of these rights and when, if ever, their defense can be suspended in favor of other moral rights or principles.

Wall's view that sexual harassment is wrong because it is a type of wrongful communication fits best the hostile work environment type of sexual harassment. However, as we will see, Wall believes it applies to all forms of sexual harassment. He offers a "set of necessary and jointly sufficient conditions of sexual harassment" that both define sexual harassment and identify what is morally wrong with it (X and Y are variables that can be replaced with people's names):

1. X successfully communicates to Y, X's or someone else's purported sexual interest in someone (whether Y or someone else).
2. Y does not consent to discuss or consider such a message about X's or someone else's purported sexual interest in someone.
3. Disregarding the absence of Y's consent, X repeats a message of this form to Y.
4. Y feels emotionally distressed because of X's disregard for the absence of Y's consent to discuss or consider such a message and/or because Y objects to the content of X's sexual comments. (Wall, "Sexual Harassment," 531)

When all four conditions are met, X has sexually harassed Y. The actions that constitute sexual harassment are all a form of communication, so sexual harassment is a type of *wrongful* communication.

Wall wants us to take the "sexual interest" referred to in the first condition broadly. For example, X's message does not need to imply a sexual attraction for Y by X or anyone else. The message only needs to have sexual content. Therefore, Jennifer's conversations with her employees about sex fulfill this condition. Wall also probably intends to be broad when it comes to the medium of communication. A message with sexual content can be communicated verbally or in writing, and both of these can take various forms: face-to-face communication, a letter, an e-mail, a post-it note, etc. Messages can also be communicated through photographs, drawings, gestures (for example, a body movement that simulates sexual intercourse), and even looks (for example, ogling).

What makes these messages wrong, according to Wall, is not their content, but that they are communicated without the consent of their receiver: "What is inherently repulsive about sexual harassment is not the possible vulgarity of X's sexual comment or proposal, but X's failure to show respect for Y's rights" (Wall, "Definition," 74). The second condition captures this aspect of sexual harassment: the receiver of the message does not consent to receive further messages of this sort. Her lack of consent can be communicated in a variety of ways: she can simply say that she does not want to receive any more messages with sexual content,[8] and she can also communicate this in writing, through a gesture, or even through what Wall calls a "suggestive silence" (Wall, "Sexual Harassment," 532). The last is a very common way we communicate to someone that we do not approve of his message or decline participating in a conversation with him; silence can sometimes communicate an even more severe objection to a message than a verbal expression.

Wall's third condition is met when someone persists in communicating messages with a sexual content even though their receiver has expressed his or her disapproval of them. According to Wall, harassment occurs only when the offending act is repeated. While a one-time sexual comment might bother its recipient and even, Wall acknowledges, violate her moral rights, "*harassment* suggests that a victim is actually hounded by a perpetrator" (Wall, "Sexual Harassment," 531). Wall's third condition is about the meaning of "harassment," and not the severity of the offense. Depending on such things as its content, a sexual message delivered once might be "more morally repugnant" than a series of different sexual messages, but "the one-time offense does not constitute harassment" (531).[9] Harassment, according to Wall, requires repetition.

There might in fact be a person who is indifferent to sexual messages. Because of this indifference, she expresses neither her consent nor her dissent to such messages being communicated to her (imagine a co-worker of Roger's who just deletes the e-mails of their supervisor and ignores her remarks). According to Wall, this person has not been harassed. Wall's fourth condition is meant to distinguish this person from someone who has been harassed. The recipient of the messages must feel some emotional distress because of either the content of the messages or their being delivered against her objections.

Wall might also intend his fourth condition to balance the rights of free expression with those that are violated by sexual harassment. It is widely accepted that restrictions on our moral rights are sometimes permissible, in particular when the exercise of a right harms others. For example, while we have the right to travel freely (for example, from home to work or school), other rights restrict it. I cannot cut through my neighbor's property; I also cannot drive over the speed limit or while intoxicated. Doing any of these things would infringe upon others' rights. I also have a right to express myself, but that can also be restricted if it entails harm to others. Now, can speech ever actually have this effect, or at least enough to warrant limiting someone's right to free expression?[10]

Many people, including Wall, believe it can.[11] But they would hold that merely being bothered by a message (as we are, for example, by those delivered by a loud talker or someone who bores us) does not entail a violation of our rights. We are often bothered by or in some other way dislike another's exercise of his or her rights without actually being harmed. The violation of someone's rights by the sexual harasser's messages, however, warrants limiting the rights of the harasser to express himself.

What rights are violated by sexual harassment? According to Wall, someone who is subjected to sexual messages against her will might have her *privacy rights* violated. Such a person is being encouraged to participate in a conversation in which information that she would rather keep private might be revealed. This information can be revealed, or at least inferences about this information can be made, even if she does not *say* anything. The harasser might ask the victim a prying yes/no question of the sort that a failure to respond can be inferred to be an affirmative response (for example, "Have you ever cheated on your spouse?"). The victim might feel compelled to participate in the conversation in order to forestall any such inferences, even if they are unjustified. Wall nevertheless acknowledges that a person's right to privacy is not always violated when the four conditions are met, describing sexual harassment as a "potential encroachment on a victim's privacy rights" (Wall, "Sexual Harassment," 534). The victim might not reveal any information about herself to the person communicating sexual messages, either resisting the pressure to do so or because this pressure is not very strong. Also, she might not consider the information she reveals to be private; it is information about herself that she shares with others without any sort of pressure.

A right that is always violated when the four conditions are met, according to Wall, is the victim's right to make autonomous choices. Wall describes this as the "fundamental fault" of sexual harassment (Wall, "Sexual Harassment," 534). The harasser has ignored the victim's lack of consent to the sexual messages and by doing so has violated her right to choose not to be subjected to such messages. We can expand on Wall's analysis again by noticing another way in which a victim's autonomy is violated. We should be allowed to choose the types of relationships we have with others. Relationships are partly constituted by the amount and kind of information the partners in the relationship share with each other; what one discloses to a friend is typically different from what one discloses to a co-worker. Jennifer, by sharing with her employees information about her sexual life—and potentially compelling them to share similar information about themselves—forces them into a relationship with her that they might not have chosen to enter.[12]

Wall's understanding of the wrongness of sexual harassment can be classified generally in the category of what I will call **dignity theories** of sexual harassment.[13] Dignity theories take the wrongness of sexual harassment to be an attack on the rights and other characteristics of persons that constitute their dignity. According to the legal scholar Rosa Ehrenreich,

> The most fundamental harm of sexual harassment is a *dignitary harm*: by humiliating, intimidating, tormenting, pressuring, or mocking individuals in their places of work, sexual harassment is an insult to the dignity, autonomy, and personhood of each victim;

such harassment violates each individual's right to be treated with
the respect and concern that is due to her as a full and equally
valuable human being. (Ehrenreich, 16; italics in original)

The point of calling sexual harassment a "dignitary harm" is to
emphasize that it is harm that can be suffered by any individual,
regardless of his or her sex. Sexual harassment violates the rights that
everyone possesses simply by virtue of being a human. Thus there
does not need to be discrimination in order for sexual harassment
to occur; discrimination, according to Ehrenreich, is the "*context in
which the harm of harassment occurs*," and not "the *nature of the
harm of harassment*" (Ehrenreich, 3; italics in original).

A dignity approach to sexual harassment can be found in certain
legal systems other than that of the United States. Whereas the focus
in U.S. sexual harassment law is equality, German law conceptualizes
sexual harassment as an attack on a person's dignity. Dignity is the
first and—as many see it—the most fundamental right in the German
Constitution, or Basic Law (*Grundgesetz*).[14] As Susanne Baer explains,
"German law defines sexual harassment as intentional, definitely of a
sexual nature, and at least in part recognizably rejected—or proven
unwelcome—activity that violates the dignity of individuals at work"
(Baer, 590). French law similarly treats sexual harassment as primarily
an attack on an individual that is harmful and violates her autonomy.[15]
For there to be discrimination, there must be unequal treatment of
the victim. Neither the moral approach of a dignity theory nor these
legal approaches require unequal treatment; only the violation of certain individual rights is necessary for sexual harassment.

Since dignity approaches to sexual harassment do not take its
harm to be discrimination, they are able to recognize the relevant
behavior of the "equal opportunity harasser" as sexual harassment.
According to Ehrenreich, "It is important to realize that workplace
harassment ... injures the dignitary interests of individual harassment
victims, regardless of their sex and regardless of the sex of their harassers" (Ehrenreich, 8). So, according to this approach, Roger has been
harassed by Jennifer. His rights to privacy and autonomy have been

violated; he has also been offended, humiliated, and possibly even intimidated by the conversations in which his supervisor has compelled him to participate.

Despite its greater inclusiveness in this respect than discrimination-based accounts of sexual harassment, some have found problems with the dignity approach generally, and Wall's theory specifically. While this need not be the case with other versions of the dignity approach, Wall's definition of sexual harassment does not cover quid pro quo cases.[16] His third condition requires that the sexual message be repeated. A case in which an employer threatens an employee *once* with firing if she does not grant him sexual favors is widely considered—including by United States law—as sexual harassment. But since it is not repeated, Wall does not consider it to be sexual harassment. He finds such behavior to be morally wrong (Wall, "Reply," 239), but he does not believe it should be *called* sexual harassment.

Another possible problem with Wall's approach and applications of dignity theories such as we find in German law is the rejection requirement. As we discussed earlier, employees can be reasonably reluctant to communicate their lack of consent to a sexual message. Among other things, they can fear retaliation for doing so.[17] However, the silent harassee is nevertheless harassed. Because of her silence, the harasser might not know that his messages are causing emotional distress; his ignorance might mitigate his culpability somewhat, but it cannot relieve him of responsibility if he should have known that his messages would cause distress. There are types of message that anyone should know are capable of causing emotional distress in another, in particular, messages that directly insult or demean another person. Wall's central example is of a message that communicates a sexual interest in the recipient. Sexual interest might be reciprocated, so a message of this sort could be welcomed by the recipient. The sender of the message might be unable to assess the degree of welcomeness until he sends the message. However, very few people would welcome the sort of messages that frequently figure in hostile work environment lawsuits.

In *Andrews v. City of Philadelphia* (1990), two female police officers successfully sued the city over a hostile work environment.[18]

They described a workplace in which they had to endure sexist and demeaning remarks. Their male co-workers sometimes continued the harassment beyond the workplace, making obscene phone calls to the female officers' homes. The "messages" their co-workers sent them also included destruction of their personal property and sometimes even physical violence. One plaintiff had her car scratched and some clothing destroyed. The other plaintiff had her tires slashed and a lime substance was placed in a shirt that was hanging in her locker, causing serious burns to her back when she put it on. In a case heard by the New Jersey Supreme Court, *Lehmann v. Toys 'R' Us, Inc.* (1993), the court found a hostile work environment that consisted of a supervisor repeatedly touching female employees in sexual ways, including lifting up their clothing.[19] Most people do not need their recipients' dissent to these sorts of messages to know that they would not be welcome.

In their rulings, the courts in these cases and others have applied what is known as the **reasonable woman standard**. That is, they look at the situation from the victim's perspective (which, in these cases, is a woman). Looking at the situation from the perspective of a reasonable *person*, on the other hand, can ignore the different perspectives of men and women. For example, in *Robinson v. Jacksonville Shipyards* (1991), the court ruled that a hostile work environment was created by, among other things, the display of photos of nude women throughout the workplace. From the perspective of heterosexual men, not only might there be nothing wrong with these photos, but they could also be seen to improve the workplace. From the perspective of women, however, they contribute to a hostile work environment; they express and reinforce the view that women should be evaluated only in terms of their worth as sex objects. In the case that established the reasonable woman standard, *Ellison v. Brady* (1991),[20] the court identified another difference between men's and women's perspectives: since women tend to be victims of sexual assault more often than men, women would be more concerned than men over unwelcome sexual attention.[21] The court acknowledged that the reasonable woman standard will change over time as the views of most women change, but the standard will always exclude the perspectives of the "rare hyper-sensitive" employee.

Some might see it as an advantage of Wall's approach that it can accommodate the perspectives of even this employee, who despite her rarity would still be emotionally distressed by unwelcome messages. However, this flexibility might be at the cost of another problem with Wall's approach. It appears that the content of the messages in cases of wrongful communication (such as sexual harassment) is ultimately unimportant. We can see this by imagining Roger's harasser to be his co-worker Charlie and substituting occurrences of "sex" or "sexual" in Wall's conditions with "taxidermy" (for example, "Y does not consent to discuss or consider such a message about X's or someone else's purported interest in *taxidermy*"). There does not seem to be anything in Wall's analysis that would make such substitutions unreasonable. Once we make them, Charlie's forcing Roger to listen to descriptions of his taxidermy would be an example of *wrongful communication* (we might call it *taxidermy* harassment, instead of sexual harassment). Charlie's messages do cause Roger emotional distress, and the same rights are violated by them as in cases of sexual harassment. Charlie does not respect Roger's right to choose not to be exposed to descriptions of taxidermy. Roger's privacy rights are violated since he is compelled to share his personal views about animal rights in expressing his dissent to Charlie's communications about taxidermy. These are views that he would rather not share with his co-workers.

However, while the messages of a sexual harasser seem to be different in kind and severity from those of a taxidermy harasser, Wall's analysis does not identify anything especially egregious about unwelcome messages that have sexual content. Also, while Wall's conditions may identify what is wrong with Jennifer's behavior toward Roger (as well as Charlie's behavior toward Roger), they do not identify any difference between that and the same behavior directed by a man against a woman. However, as the court in *Ellison v. Brady* recognized, men's and women's perspectives are different to the extent that a sexual message directed toward a man (for example, the display of pornographic pictures) will often mean something different when directed toward a woman.

The philosopher Elizabeth Anderson has noticed this problem with the dignity approach in general; she argues that it "individualizes and depoliticizes the harm of sexual harassment" (Anderson, 294). By conceiving of sexual harassment as a dignity harm to indivduals, the dignity approach ignores the context that allows us to see all the harms it causes to women. The dignity approach, for example, makes it difficult to see the women exposed to and distressed by the photographs at the Jacksonville Shipyards as "reasonable women," that is, as anything other than prudes, overly self-conscious women, or "shrews" intent on ruining the men's good times. Approaches that take sexual harassment to be a kind of gender discrimination, however, are capable of accounting for the entire context of the harassing behavior.

SEXUAL HARASSMENT AS DISCRIMINATION

The most influential and famous advocate of the view that the wrongness of sexual harassment consists of its being a kind of gender discrimination is Catherine MacKinnon. As discussed in Chapter One, MacKinnon's writings and advocacy on behalf of this view influenced United States law on sexual harassment, which views it as type of gender discrimination.[22] In her seminal book *Sexual Harassment of Working Women*, MacKinnon writes, "Working conditions that differ by sex are sex discriminatory" (210). The (heterosexual) sexual harasser selects his victims based on their sex. While not all members of the victim's sex might be selected, her sex is nevertheless a primary reason for her selection. The working conditions of a victim of sexual harassment are different from those of employees of the other sex: she or he is expected to comply with demands for sexual favors or tolerate a working environment in which she or he is in other ways demeaned. As MacKinnon explains for situations in which sexual harassment is directed at women, sexual harassment "creates two employment standards: one for women that includes sexual requirements, one for men that does not" (MacKinnon, *Sexual Harassment*, 193). Sexual harassment is wrong, according to MacKinnon's view, because it discriminates in this way on the basis of gender.

MacKinnon's views about the wrongness of sexual harassment, along with others that see it as being discrimination, can be classified with what I will call **equality theories** of sexual harassment.[23] In contrast to dignity theories, which see sexual harassment as resulting in an injury to an individual, equality theories see sexual harassment as causing a *group* injury. People suffer the harms of sexual harassment because of their membership in a group, namely, their sex. The effect of sexual harassment is to weaken the social position of that group, and thus that of the individual members of that group. Unlike Wall's theory, equality theories can specify what is especially egregious about sexual messages that create a hostile work environment. It is not only—if even—that they are delivered without the consent of the recipient; the content of the messages is also important. Sexual messages express and reinforce the subordination of the sex to which they are directed. Equality theories are also able to recognize the special harm caused to women by sexual harassment. As one advocate of the equality approach puts it, sexual harassment is "a technology of sexism" (Franke, 693). When women are the victims, sexual harassment is an extension of the subjugation of women outside the workplace. MacKinnon argues that women have always "been required to exchange sexual services for material survival, in one form or another" (MacKinnon, *Sexual Harassment*, 174). Historically, this exchange occurred in marriage or prostitution, both of which, according to MacKinnon, "in different ways institutionalize this arrangement" (175). When women entered the labor force in large numbers in the last century, this did not offer them freedom from this exchange; instead, "the sexual standard they were judged by accompanied them" (175). Proponents of the equality approach see increased public acceptance of the wrongness of sexual harassment as a means by which women can finally escape this sexual standard.

A further way in which equality theories differ from dignity theories such as Wall's is in not placing as much emphasis on emotional distress and consent. Wall takes emotional distress caused by sexual messages and their recipient's lack of consent to them to be necessary conditions for sexual harassment. However, sexual harassment can cause other injuries besides emotional distress, in particular, economic injury. It can compel the victim to quit her job, it might impede her professional advancement, and it can affect her chances of receiving raises and cause her other economic injuries. These harms persist even if sexual harassment causes relatively little direct emotional distress. Vaughana Macy Feary argues that "women have been conditioned to stoically accept a great deal of sexual behavior which may harm them professionally" (Feary, 655–56). This culturally enforced stoicism might also reveal itself in women's reluctance to express their dissent to hostile work environments. We have already seen how all employees can be inhibited from expressing dissent to sexual messages because of a fear of suffering economic injuries. Feary is suggesting another explanation for this reluctance on the part of women.

Other employees may be harmed aside from the immediate victims of sexual harassment. We can call them **third-party employees**. In workplaces in which quid pro quo harassment is rife, people not directly targeted with sexual demands may be harmed. They are being denied employment benefits, but not because of any of their employment-related characteristics. I explore this issue further in the next section. If there is a practice in a workplace of making job benefits conditional upon the fulfillment of sexual demands, this can create a hostile work environment that also harms others aside from the direct target of those demands.[24] If only one sex is the target of sexual demands, then such a practice functions like pornographic pictures displayed in a workplace. It implies that one sex is to be judged according to a sexual standard.

Equality theories broaden the range of victims of sexual harassment beyond its direct victims and third-party employees. According to MacKinnon, sexual harassment is a "social wrong and social injury" (MacKinnon, *Sexual Harassment*, 175). Insofar as sexual harassment is an extension of discriminatory practices against women outside the workplace and helps sustain those practices, then all women are victims of sexual harassment. Every case of sexual harassment against women perpetuates the sexual standard by which women are judged in and out of the workplace.

On the other hand, all men are not necessarily the victims of individual acts of sexual harassment targeted against men. Men are situated differently than women in a male-dominated society. It might be that cases of sexual harassment of men cause some erosion to male dominance, but they do not perpetuate practices of discrimination against men. However, some versions of the equality approach hold that since they are not part of a practice of discrimination, unwanted sexual advances and similar acts against men do not count as sexual harassment.

I have already discussed one problem with the view that sexual harassment is wrong because it is discriminatory: it has difficulty accounting for the wrongness of equal-opportunity sexual harassment. Wall and others have offered their alternative dignity approaches, in part, to explain why this and other types of sexual harassment are wrong. According to their approaches, we can see what is wrong with the way Roger is treated by his supervisor. However, some advocates of the equality approach do not believe that an alternative approach is required. They disagree, for example, with the U.S. Supreme Court in *Oncale v. Sundowner Offshore Services, Inc.* (1998) that men can be the victims of sexual harassment. Jan Crosthwaite and Graham Priest argue that "women cannot commit [sexual harassment], nor men be victims" (68). Crosthwaite and Priest hold that sexual harassment is a form of oppression, which is "a relation between social groups which involves one group wielding power which is illegitimate, in some sense, over another group in the society" (66). Sexual harassment is "a pattern of sexual behavior that constitutes or contributes to the oppression of one gender group by another" (66). Since men are the dominant sex in our society, Crosthwaite and Priest conclude, only men can sexually harass and only women can be their victims. Only in a society in which women were the dominant sex could women be sexual harassers.[25]

If Crosthwaite and Priest are correct, then Roger is not a victim of sexual harassment. This would still be the case if Jennifer were not an equal-opportunity harasser, and also if she were a man. However, Sandra Levitsky tries to accommodate cases such as Roger's into her account of sexual harassment, while maintaining the view that sexual harassment is a form of gender oppression. It is such because it reinforces gender stereotypes, which work by making differences between men and women in our society seem natural and universal. The gender stereotypes of our culture ultimately benefit the men: they portray men as possessing characteristics that make them capable of assuming dominant roles in society, and they portray women as lacking those characteristics and instead possessing ones incompatible with such roles. So, given their power to influence how we treat other people, gender stereotypes have the specific effect of causing us to treat women as naturally subordinate to men. The reinforcement of gender stereotypes adds to men's power over women. As Levitsky explains, "Preserving gender distinctions goes hand in hand with preserving the rewards men derive from these distinctions" (219). Jennifer's behavior toward Roger (as well as a male harasser's behavior toward him) is sexual harassment because it reinforces these stereotypes: "When a person sexually harasses a man, the harasser both feminizes him and reinforces the idea that those qualities associated with women are subordinate to the qualities associated with men" (Levitsky, 219). The legal scholar Katherine M. Franke explains how this is discrimination: "... sexual harassment is a kind of sex discrimination [because] it perpetuates, enforces, and polices a set of gender norms that seek to feminize women and masculinize men" (696). Franke is thinking of sexual harassment directed against women. According to Levitsky, sexual harassment directed against men entails their feminization by making them subordinate; this is to impose upon them qualities that the gender stereotypes attribute to women.

In addition to same-sex and equal-opportunity sexual harassment, this version of an equality approach comprehends the harassment of gays and lesbians because of their sexual orientation. Anti-gay harassment acts as a form of gender-policing; its victims are being harassed because of their failure to conform to gender stereotypes. Like the other forms of sexual harassment, it has the effect of preserving "the differences between the sexes as well as the hierarchy which forms the basis of sex discrimination" (Levitsky, 219). However, while the equality approach of Levitsky does allow us to see sexual harassment in cases like Roger's, it does not take the male target of any of these forms of sexual harassment to be its victim. Since they are men, they actually benefit from the reinforcement of stereotypes. All women, instead, are the victims of the sexually harassing behavior. So, Levitsky's approach would suggest, when Jennifer "harasses" Roger, her actions actually victimize her and benefit Roger.

Crosthwaite and Priest may be correct that sexual harassment is a form of oppression and thus a means by which one sex oppresses the other. That does not preclude it from also being a means by which one individual harms another individual. Slavery is oppression, but it is also a harm against an individual, and that harm can be caused outside of any particular system of societal oppression (for example, a white man enslaving another white man). Levitsky and Franke might also be correct that sexual harassment enforces gender stereotypes that contribute to the power of men in society. But that should not prevent us from seeing the different harms caused to someone like Roger by acts of sexual harassment.

SEXUAL HARASSMENT AND THE AT-WILL DOCTRINE

People have tended to favor either the equality or the dignity approach to sexual harassment to the exclusion of the other. However, there is another option, which is to see *both* as identifying something wrong with sexual harassment. It is true, as dignity theories see it, that sexual harassment is an attack on a person's dignity; it violates a person's rights to privacy and autonomy, among others. These attacks can be made against men or women, and they can be made by either sex as well. Sexual harassment can also be a form of gender discrimination, as equality theories see it. When women are the victims, sexual harassment is part of a pattern of discrimination that women face both in and outside the workplace, the school, and other institutions. As such, it helps sustain the subordination of women in society. While men can also be the victims of gender discrimination, the harms to them are not all the same and not part of a general pattern of discrimination that exists outside the workplace.

As a policy matter, changes to the law might be required to cover both sorts of harms. As discussed above, United States law has adopted a version of the equality theory that does not recognize the equal-opportunity harasser. Also, while some equality approaches recognize harassment of gays and lesbians as sexual harassment, United States law has yet to do so. Below I will discuss a change to the law that can include all the kinds of sexual harassment discussed so far. As a moral matter, however, we can recognize both sorts of harm; we need not choose between the dignity and equality approaches.

What have been described as problems with these approaches are actually just examples of their incompleteness. We need both approaches to explain everything that is wrong with sexual harassment. However, these two approaches are not enough. There is at least one other harm caused by sexual harassment for which neither accounts. Despite the focus of their advocates on workplace harassment, neither approach recognizes the particular harm that harassment can have in the workplace. To understand this harm, it is necessary to understand the nature of the employment relationship for most people in the United States, as well as many other places.

For most employees in the United States, the employee-employer relationship is governed by the **at-will doctrine**. In the absence of an explicit contract, the employee is free to quit whenever she wants, and the employer is free to fire the employee whenever she wants. Neither party needs to have a good reason for ending the employment relationship. The employer's right is often stated as the right to fire an employee for good cause, bad cause, or no cause at all.[26] Courts have recognized some exceptions to the at-will doctrine since it was first articulated in 1884. There are *public policy* exceptions to the doctrine; for example, an employee cannot be fired for refusing to do something illegal. There are statutory exceptions, such as those established by Title VII of the Civil Rights Act of 1964, which prohibits firing someone because of his or her race, color, religion, sex, or national origin; subsequent legislation has added protections for age and disability.[27] Other than these and a few other exceptions, an at-will employee can be fired at any time and for any, or no, reason.[28] Most other industrialized nations follow some version of a *just cause* doctrine, which requires employers to have a good reason for firing an employer.

Employees work in order to receive a paycheck. For every job, there are certain prescribed duties, as well as standards as to how well those duties must be fulfilled. It is assumed, if never made explicit, that an employee must perform these duties according to these standards in order to keep her job and receive her paycheck. These are the employer's minimum expectations. However, many workers will try to exceed these expectations by performing their duties to a higher standard, as well as taking on duties that are not explicitly assigned to them. Their motivations for doing so are the various job benefits beyond a paycheck, such as raises, promotions, and bonuses. Unlike a paycheck, these are not received—it is typically assumed— by merely doing the minimum. The employee who does more than is expected is more deserving of these benefits than an employee who simply does the minimum. However, if a supervisor does not take an employee's extra efforts into account, and instead gives benefits to employees who do not put in any extra effort, then the employee has performed the extra duties for nothing. This is what can happen in a workplace where there is sexual harassment. Employees are not evaluated on their work-related characteristics, but instead on their sexuality or their willingness to tolerate a hostile work environment. The employees who work harder are being harmed because they are essentially working for free. Their extra effort is not compensated by the job benefits they had reasonably expected to accrue to them; the employees put in this extra effort only on the assumption that it will figure into fair and relevant evaluations of them.

Some might say that an employee in such a workplace simply should not put in any extra effort, since she knows that she will not receive any extra job benefits because of it. But among the benefits that an employee expects to receive is continual employment. For at-will employees, the employment relationship is a tenuous one, so they can be motivated to put in extra effort simply in order to preserve their jobs. In fact, employees have a stronger motivation to be a good employee than an employer has to be a good employer. It is typically harder to find a new job than it is to find a new employee, especially an employee for an at-will job. But unless the employer takes this effort into account when deciding whether to keep the employee or grant her extra job benefits, he is getting more out of the employee than what he is paying her to do. Despite their best efforts, employees might lose their job or not get a promotion, but as long as the employer judged them only on their work-related characteristics, they are still compensated in a way for their extra work. It was at least not done entirely for nothing.

This asymmetry in the employee-employer relationship, which grants the employer greater power and autonomy, creates a workplace environment in which sexual harassment can flourish. As legal scholar Lea Vander Velde explains, "it is not gender alone that has rendered employees vulnerable to unwelcome sexual approaches. It is also coercive circumstances of the at-will doctrine under which employers and managers enjoy virtually unlimited prerogatives to dismiss employees" (Vander Velde, 501). At-will employees do not have sufficient power to resist sexual harassment; instead, they have incentive not only to tolerate it but also to accept it, while still doing their jobs well.

Philosopher James P. Sterba argues that employers have a moral obligation to follow what he calls the "Principle of Desert": it requires employers to "treat and evaluate people on the basis of their proper role- or job-related qualifications and excellences when this is appropriate or required" (Sterba, 240). This principle is not followed in a workplace in which there is sexual harassment; employees are evaluated on their sexuality, rather than their work-related characterstics. However, increased acceptance of our obligation to this principle might reduce occurences of sexual harassment.[29] Further relaxing the at-will doctrine or changing to a just cause system would do more. These steps would also reduce other kinds of harassment in the workplace that are not covered by existing legislation. Adoption of a just cause doctrine would best protect employees from the variety of harms that the workplace can engender, and it would ensure that Sterba's principle of desert is followed. Employees would then be compensated for all the labor they perform for an employer.

SUMMARY

Generally, there are two ways of conceiving of the wrongness of sexual harassment, with variations under each approach. According to dignity theories, sexual harassment is a dignity harm. It is behavior that "tends to humiliate, torment, threaten, intimidate, pressure, demean, frighten, or injure the person to whom it is directed" (Ehrenreich, 15). Equality theories, on the other hand, see sexual harassment as a group harm. The specific harm its victims suffer is discrimination; they are denied various job benefits because of gender. Advocates of the equality approach fault the dignity approach for individualizing the harm of sexual harassment; they argue that it fails to see how sexual harassment helps sustain societal gender inequality. Equality theories, on the other hand, have difficulty identifying the harm caused by the equal-opportunity harasser.

It is possible to accept both approaches as identifying something wrong with sexual harassment. A supplement to their approaches recognizes the harm caused by sexual harassment in the context of employment, especially at-will employment. Employees will typically work to exceed the expectations of their employers, especially the at-will employee, who does so not only for the sake of various employment benefits, but also in order to preserve her job. At-will employees are more vulnerable to sexual harassment. Relaxation of the doctrine, or conversion to a just cause doctrine, would protect employees from sexual and other sorts of workplace harassment.

REVIEW QUESTIONS
1. What is an equal-opportunity harasser?
2. How is sexual harassment a kind of wrongful communication, according to Edmund Wall?

3. What are the differences between dignity and equality theories of sexual harassment?
4. What is the reasonable woman standard?
5. What is the employment at-will doctrine?

DISCUSSION QUESTIONS

1. Is the equal-opportunity harasser a sexual harasser?
2. Do both the equality and dignity approaches identify something wrong with sexual harassment? Is there anything else wrong with sexual harassment?
3. Do laws against hostile work environments violate free-speech rights?
4. Can men be the victims of sexual harassment?
5. Should the employment at-will doctrine be abandoned, or are the common-law and statutory exceptions enough to protect the rights of employees and employers?

GROUP ACTIVITIES

1. Come up with a list of harms caused by sexual harassment, and then discuss answers to these questions: a) which should be illegal to commit? b) how many are harms to dignity? c) how many are group-based injuries? d) are some suffered only by women (or men)?
2. In small groups, identify possible changes to United States sexual harassment law that would encompass "equal-opportunity" harassment. These changes can include new legislation or different interpretations of existing law. As a full group, discuss the merits and demerits of each proposal.

NOTES

1 I have explored the topic of this chapter elsewhere in a very different forum; see Dromm.

2 *Oncale v. Sundowner Offshore Services, Inc.*, 523 U.S. 75 (1998).

3 *Holman v. Indiana*, 211 F.3d 399 (Court of Appeals, 7th Cir. 2000).

4 In another case from 2000, a different appeals court decided against a woman who claimed sexual harassment because, among other things, her

supervisor used foul language (*Hocevar v. Purdue Frederick, Co.*, 223 F.3d 721 [Court of Appeals, 8th Cir. 2000]). Since the supervisor used this language in front of all his employees, it could not be considered sexual harassment: "The use of foul language in front of both men and women is not discrimination based on sex."

5 At least, they cannot sue Jennifer or their company for sexual harassment.

6 So, in the previous chapter, we could have talked about the violation of Sara's moral rights by sexual harassment even though we could not, as we discussed, talk about the violation of her legal rights.

7 The establishment of legal rights is also complicated, but in a different sort of way. There are many ways in which legal rights can be established—for example, through legislation, executive decree, or the decisions of courts or common law. It is also important to recognize that the establishment of these rights is often related to their prior recognition as moral rights.

8 She might object generally to messages with sexual content, or just to messages with certain sexual content (e.g., those that express X's sexual interest in her); or she can object to messages with sexual content delivered by a particular person.

9 While Wall believes that his philosophical definition of sexual harassment should have some influence on its legal definition (he rejects the EEOC definition), there is nothing to suggest that he would not support laws or some other sort of legal remedy against these other forms of sexual messages.

10 The legal issue was addressed by the court in *Robinson v. Jacksonville Shipyards, Inc.* (760 F. Supp. 1486 [M.D. Fla. 1991]). The court concluded that pornographic pictures and verbal harassment are not protected speech because they are discriminatory acts constituting a hostile work environment. The court said such speech is indistinguishable from other sorts of speech that constitute a crime, such as the speech used in threats or blackmail.

11 Others disagree; see, for example, Browne.

12 Wall might also want to say that, given his fourth condition, sexual harassment violates the victim's right not to be emotionally distressed. Elsewhere, Wall says that sexual harassment is, as an "unjustified harm," a kind of abuse that "may include various ways of inflicting psychological harm" (Wall, "Definition," 73).

13 This is the term Elizabeth Anderson uses for a group of normative theories about sexual harassment that she discusses (Anderson). I'm also using her term for the next category of theories I discuss, equality theories. However, Anderson identifies several other categories of theory. I am using these two terms more broadly, so they include some of Anderson's other categories.

14 Dignity is not mentioned in the United States constitution.

15 See Saguy. Interestingly, the hostile work environment type of sexual harassment is not recognized by French law.

16 See Landau ("Repetition" and "Wrongful") for this and some other
    criticisms of Wall.

17 Recall that the U.S. Supreme Court in *Meritor Savings Bank v. Vinson*
    (1986) held that the unwelcomeness of the behavior, rather than the victim's
    consent to it, was all that was necessary for sexual harassment.

18 *Andrews v. City of Philadelphia*, 895 F.2d 1469 (Court of Appeals, 3rd Cir.
    1990).

19 *Lehmann v. Toys 'R' Us, Inc.*, 132 N.J. 587 (1993).

20 *Ellison v. Brady*, 924 F.2d 872 (Court of Appeals, 9th Cir.1991).

21 This has been supported by research in the social sciences. For example, one
    group of researchers report that "women are more likely to perceive that
    harassment has taken place and typically rate the behavior as more severe,
    inappropriate, and offensive than do men" (Willness, Steel, and Lee, 152).

22 MacKinnon's views on hate speech and pornography have had a similar
    influence on Canadian law. These are discussed in the Conclusion of this
    book.

23 In the *Sexual Harassment of Women*, MacKinnon actually offers two
    accounts of the discriminatory nature of sexual harassment (both of which
    I intend my *equality theory* label to encompass); one she calls the "equality"
    approach, and the other she calls the "differences" approach. She prefers
    the former but anticipates, correctly, that the latter would be adopted by the
    courts. The "equality" approach takes sexual harassment to be one example
    of the social inequality of men and women, such that it "sees women's
    situation as a structural problem of enforced inferiority that needs to be
    radically altered" (MacKinnon, *Sexual Harassment*, 5). According to the
    "differences" approach, the wrongness of sexual harassment consists of its
    treating women differently, and injuriously, from men.

24 Alba Conte discusses one such case, *Broderick v. Ruder* (685 F. Supp. 1269
    [D.D.C. 1988]), and concludes, "Even a woman who was never herself the
    object of harassment might have a Title VII claim if she were forced to
    work in an atmosphere in which such harassment was pervasive" (59).

25 For another argument that reaches this conclusion, see Superson.

26 This is a paraphrase of a remark in a court decision that first articulated the
    at-will doctrine: "All [employers] may dismiss their employees at will, ... for
    good cause, for no cause, or even for cause morally wrong, without thereby
    being guilty of a legal wrong" (*Payne v. Western & Atlantic R. R. Co.*, 81
    Tenn. 507 [1884]).

27 The Age Discrimination in Employment Act (1967) and the Americans with
    Disabilities Act (1990).

28 Recognition of these exceptions to the doctrine actually varies from state to
    state, but Montana passed legislation in 1987 that entirely abandoned the
    at-will doctrine: the Wrongful Discharge from Employment Act.

29 Ethical discussions of sexual harassment, such as the present one, are
    intended to have this effect.

CHAPTER 3

Where Can Sexual Harassment Occur?

Marie works in a downtown office building. She walks to and from work every day. The route she takes between her apartment and her office building is twelve blocks in each direction. For the last few months, a construction site has been at the middle of this route. Almost every time she walks by it, some of the men working there have directed wolf whistles and catcalls at her. The latter consist of sexual invitations and shouted comments about her physical appearance, and the language in which they make these comments is obscene, explicit, and vulgar. The construction site will be there for another several months. Marie is contemplating taking another route to work in order to avoid the construction site; this will add another three blocks to her route.

As the title of the chapter indicates, we are interested here in *where* sexual harassment can occur. So far, we have focused on sexual harassment in the workplace, but sexual harassment can occur in other contexts such as schools. Professional relationships provide another context in which sexual harassment poses a particular danger. For this, and other reasons, professional organizations for physicians, psychologists, lawyers, and others have ethics codes that prohibit sexual relationships with clients. I begin this chapter by examining the ethics codes of these organizations and discussing the reasons for such prohibitions. As is the case in workplaces and schools, professional relationships often contain disparities in power; therefore, harassment in these relationships is capable of satisfying the third condition of the core definition of sexual harassment that we arrived at in Chapter One. The second part of this chapter examines whether this condition can be satisfied elsewhere, for example, in situations like Marie's. We ask whether sexual harassment can occur outside of workplaces, schools, and professional relationships. The chapter concludes by examining whether a disparity in power should be a necessary condition of sexual harassment.

SEXUAL HARASSMENT IN THE PROFESSIONS

The codes of ethics of various professional organizations prohibit sexual relationships between members of the organization and their clients or patients. There are various reasons for prohibiting such relationships. For example, they can detract from the efficacy of the relationship: a physician who is sexually involved with a patient might be incapable of making the best objective decisions about her treatment. A lawyer's sexual or romantic interest in a client can jeopardize the latter's interests in analogous ways. But aside from consensual sexual relationships, another danger in many professional relationships is sexual harassment, particularly of the quid pro quo variety. The third condition of the core definition of sexual harassment that we arrived at in Chapter One is that the person who is responsible for the unwelcome sexual actions has power over the person who is the target of the actions. Such a power disparity often exists in professional relationships, where the person with the power can use it to obtain sexual favors from the other.

The American Medical Association's *Code of Medical Ethics* prohibits sexual relationships between physicians and patients. The code states, "Sexual contact that occurs concurrent with the patient-physician relationship constitutes sexual misconduct." It notes that physicians have an obligation, at minimum, to terminate the professional relationship before beginning a sexual relationship. However, the sexual relationship remains unethical if "the physician uses or exploits trust, knowledge, emotions, or influence derived from the previous professional relationship."[1]

The American Psychological Association's *Ethical Principles of Psychologists and Code of Conduct* has several standards related to sexual relationships between psychologists and their clients or patients. They state that psychologists "do not engage in sexual intimacies with current therapy clients/patients" and "do not accept as therapy clients/patients persons with whom they have engaged in sexual intimacies." In the case of former clients/patients, the code stipulates that they should not be initiated for "at least two years after cessation or termination of therapy" and only "in the most unusual circumstances." The psychologist "bear[s] the burden of demonstrating that there has been no exploitation" of the client/patient in light of several factors, including "any statements or actions made by the therapist during the course of therapy suggesting or inviting the possibility of a post[-]termination sexual or romantic relationship with the client/patient."[2] Other factors include the length and intensity of the therapy, the amount of time that has passed since its termination, the reasons for its termination, and the current mental status of the client/patient.

The American Bar Association's *Model Rules of Professional Conduct* states: "A lawyer shall not have sexual relations with a client unless a consensual sexual relationship existed between them when the client-lawyer relationship commenced."[3] There is no mention of whether a sexual relationship can be started following the termination of the professional relationship. State bar associations have their own rules of conduct; most follow these "model" rules. However, not all of the rules have been adopted by the states; for example, the rule regarding sexual relations with clients (1.8j) has not been adopted by the Louisiana Rules of Professional Conduct for lawyers.[4] The

New York State Bar Association prohibits more specifically only those sexual relations in which the client is in some way compelled by the lawyer to enter and those in which the lawyer is representing the client in a domestic relations matter.[5]

The Canada Bar Association has no outright ban on consensual sexual relations between lawyers and clients. Nevertheless, some provincial law societies address the issue in their codes of conduct. For example, in its *Rules of Professional Conduct*, the Law Society of Upper Canada observes that "a sexual or intimate personal relationship with a client ... may conflict with the lawyer's duty to provide objective, disinterested professional advice to the client." It advises lawyers to consider before continuing or entering into a sexual relationship with a client such factors as the "emotional and economic" vulnerability of the client; whether the relationship would create a "power imbalance in favour of the lawyer or, in some circumstances, in favour of the client"; and whether the relationship will "interfere in any way with the lawyer's fiduciary obligations to the client."[6]

Most nations' militaries prohibit sexual relationships between certain ranks, such as between officers and enlisted personnel. Prohibited relationships such as these fall under the category of **fraternization**. In contrast to the codes governing professional relationships, the violation of fraternization policies can result in a criminal penalty under military law. A physician, psychologist, or lawyer who enters a prohibited sexual relationship has done something immoral according to these codes. He or she can also face disciplinary action because of this violation, for example, disbarment or loss of license to practice medicine.

For example, in 2004, a Toronto personal injury lawyer was disbarred by the Law Society of Upper Canada for having sexual relations with a client.[7] The committee that decided on his disbarment found that he had fondled the client, entered into a consensual sexual relationship with her, and tried to continue the relationship after she told him she wanted to end it. A Florida plastic surgeon lost his medical license in the 1990s after being accused of sexually abusing several patients, including soliciting sex from them in exchange for surgeries.[8] An Air Force general was reprimanded in 2004 for numerous consensual sexual affairs, including with female officers and enlisted women. His punishment included forfeit of pay and retirement at a lower rank.[9]

Although they do not always meet the legal definitions of sexual harassment, and are not typically considered in discussions of normative definitions of it, cases of sexual harassment can occur within professional relationships. That is one of the reasons why they are prohibited. More specifically, these relationships contain the essential elements of quid pro quo harassment. The person with power in the relationship can use it to get the other to submit to sexual demands. A closer examination of power will help us understand better how it can be used to compel sexual favors from another.

POWER AND COERCION

Philosophers and others have analyzed and understood power in many different ways. The conception of power that is the focus here is the power to compel a person to do something that he or she would not want to do if it were not for the exertion of that power. When someone has this sort of power because of his or her position within an institution, we can also call it *authority*. The power of a police officer, a teacher, a supervisor, and so on, is the authority that he or she has over other individuals. However, when they use this power illegitimately, we typically say that they have acted outside of their authority. Thus, power and authority are related, but not synonymous. We can also distinguish between two sorts of power: physical and non-physical. The former is simply the use of physical strength or a weapon to compel another person to do something. For example, a police office can use her physical strength or taser gun to compel someone to stop running from her. When she does, she is exerting physical power over this individual. Non-physical power encompasses a wide variety of cases in which an individual can compel another to do something without physically compelling her to do it. Sometimes the threat of physical power can compel another to do something. A police officer shouting

"Stop or I will tase you" is an example. It is the threat of physical harm in cases like this that can motivate the person to act in a certain way. Other sorts of harms can be threatened in the use of non-physical power. A person can compel another to act by threatening to take away something they value, for example, a job. In contrast to physical power, the power in these cases is not directly over an individual's body, but over things the individual values or desires.

Quid pro quo sexual harassment always involves some sort of non-physical power. It might also involve physical power, but if it involves solely physical power then it is better classified as sexual assault or rape, rather than sexual harassment. Also, fear of physical harm—and not only being fired or demoted—can compel an employee to comply with an employer's sexual demands; as mentioned in Chapter Two, fears of sexual assault can influence a victim's perceptions of this and other types of sexual harassment.

Of course, not all uses of power are illegitimate or an abuse of power. When any sort of power is used successfully to compel someone to do something against his or her wishes, and whether it is legitimate or not, we typically call this *coercion*.[10] However, the most influential account of coercion, offered by the philosopher Robert Nozick, restricts coercion to uses of non-physical power. He provides a list of necessary and sufficient conditions for coercion, which I have simplified and adapted for our purposes:

X *coerces* Y if and only if:
1) X wants Y to do A;
2) X communicates to Y that if he does not do A, then X will do something that will make not doing A seem less desirable than doing A;
3) Y does A;
4) Part of Y's reasons for doing A is that he does not want the less desirable thing mentioned in 2).

Since quid pro quo sexual harassment always involves non-physical power, we can adopt Nozick's restriction of coercion to non-physical uses of power. Instead of physical power, coercion in Nozick's sense uses threats. In Chapter Four, I examine threats even more closely, but for now two points are worth noting. First, threats are a kind of proposal. Second, threats try to compel someone to perform an action by communicating an intention to do something to him or her that is less desirable to that person than performing the action would be. For a threat to be effective, the target of the threat must believe in its sincerity and in the power of the person making the threat to bring about those less desirable consequences. The target is coerced into performing that action when she does so because she does not want the less desirable consequences of not doing it.

In order to understand why coercion is sometimes wrong, we first need to distinguish threats from another sort of proposal: offers. Threats and offers are similar in that, being proposals, the person making them commits himself to doing something (or not doing something) if the target of the proposal performs some action (or does not perform an action). I can offer to make my friend dinner if he helps me paint my house. The difference between such an offer and a threat is that the offer makes its target *better off* (from at least the perspective of the recipient of the proposal) than he was before the offer was made. If I tell my friend that if he does not help me paint my house I will take my left-over paint and graffiti his house, I have not made him better off. I have threatened him. Threats are coercive because they compel a person to act so as to avoid being made worse off by the issuer of the threat. The issuer of the threat intervenes in another's life and commits himself to making it worse unless the other does something to benefit him.[11]

Not all uses of coercion are wrong, of course. As I previously noted, some people have authority to coerce others in performing certain actions. Let us use *authority* once again to refer to those uses of power that are in this way legitimate. A supervisor can coerce an employee into performing some job-related task by threatening to fire her if she does not.[12] When he does so, he does not act outside of his authority. However, if the supervisor threatens to fire an employee if she does not have sex with him, the supervisor is acting outside of his authority. In both cases, the recipient of the threat is made worse off by it, but only the second case—an example of quid pro quo sexual harassment—is typically considered wrong. It is wrong because the supervisor is using his power in a way that he is not entitled to use it. In fact, no one has the authority to coerce sexual behavior from another individual.

However, persons are morally free to exchange sex for various non-sexual benefits. A prostitute can exchange sex for money. A spouse can exchange sex for yard work. While such exchanges can involve coercion, it is possible they do not. Can such exchanges occur in the workplace between an employer and employee? Consider a case in which a supervisor proposes to an employee that he will promote her if she has sex with him. He tells her sincerely that there will be no negative consequences for her if she declines, and she believes him.[13] She has sex with her supervisor. Has she been coerced? The employer's proposal has not made her worse off. In fact, it has improved her situation. So, she was not *threatened* into having sex with her supervisor; her supervisor made her an *offer* that she accepted. Has she still been harmed in any way?

The philosopher David Zimmerman's concept of *coercive offers* provides a possible answer to this question. These are proposals that do not contain threats but that nevertheless coerce their recipient into performing some action. They occur when, first of all, the recipient of the offer is in a vulnerable position that makes it very difficult for him or her to refuse the offer. The offer to save a drowning person in exchange for his life savings may improve his condition, but it is an offer he really cannot refuse. However, for Zimmerman, the person making this offer is not coercing the drowning person, although he might be *exploiting* him (Zimmerman, 134ff). For Zimmerman, "a coercive offer is not merely an extremely unattractive offer *which Q cannot afford to refuse*: it is all-important *how* Q came to be in such a vulnerable position. I would claim that for P's offer to be genuinely coercive it must be the case that *he actively prevents Q from being in the alternative pre-proposal situation Q strongly prefers*" (133). A person making a threat intervenes in another's life, making that life worse when they make the threat. With coercive offers, as opposed to merely exploitative offers, this intervention takes place earlier. For example, imagine that the rescuer threw his victim into the water and then offered to rescue him in exchange for his life savings (Zimmerman, 134–35). While this offer will make the drowning person *better off*, the person making it put him into the situation requiring this rescue. The drowning person would prefer, above all else, that this person had not thrown him into the water.

It might be possible to see the sexual harasser who makes a successful sexual *offer* (as opposed to a threat) to an employee as coercing that employee. What if our employee were in line to receive a promotion but her supervisor stalls the process? She is a good worker and would likely have received a promotion but for the intervention of her supervisor. Her supervisor then tells her that he will let the promotion go through if she has sex with him. This proposal makes her better off, so it is thus an offer. However, it only makes her better off because of the supervisor's prior alteration of her situation. So, if she accepts the offer then the supervisor has coerced her, even though he did not threaten her.

However, what if our employee is unqualified for the promotion; that is, she would not get a promotion were it not for a supervisor willing to exchange it for sexual favors? Let us say that she is lazy, incompetent, and has always been indifferent about promotions. When she is offered a promotion in exchange for having sex with her supervisor, someone with whom she would otherwise not have a sexual relationship, she accepts. Has she been harmed? This exchange seems like the ones discussed a moment ago in which a person exchanges sex for a non-sexual benefit, but without being coerced into doing so. However, in the next chapter I will have more to say about a case very much like this one, but involving a professor and a student.

Coercion is an element not only in quid pro quo cases of sexual harassment; hostile work environments can also be coercive. The victims of a hostile work environment are compelled to suffer a degrading and offensive environment. The threats that coerce them to tolerate it can be explicit or implicit (a distinction I will explore thoroughly in the next chapter). The threats can be over their job benefits, as well as their job retention. The threats can also be over an increase in the severity of the hostile work environment. For those who complain about hostile work environments, the harassment often becomes worse.

The power exerted over these and all other victims of sexual harassment is more specifically exerted over things that these victims value or desire. That is what makes threats or coercive offers effective. So, we can modify the third condition of our core definition to reflect this. In the next section we will examine how this sort of power exists in various professional relationships and how it can lead to sexual harassment and other sorts of harm to the person without the power.

COERCION IN THE PROFESSIONS

In the professional relationships discussed earlier, the professional has power over various things that are valued or desired by the client or patient. These things can figure into threats that the professional could use to coerce the other into a sexual relationship. For example, a physician or psychologist has power over the health of his or her patient, and this covers a wide range of factors that can contribute to or detract from the patient's overall well-being. A lawyer may have power over his or her client's finances and, in the case of a defendant in a criminal trial, his or her freedom. These professionals also have power over confidential information revealed to them by the client or patient during the professional relationship. The threat of revealing this information can be used to coerce the other into a sexual relationship. A military officer has power over his or her subordinates that is similar to, but goes beyond, that possessed by other supervisors. He or she can determine subordinates' promotions, transfers, awards, medals, honors, and so on, and can initiate disciplinary action against them; this particular power is comparable to that of a police officer, rather than an ordinary supervisor.

In its *Rules on Professional Conduct*, the Florida Bar recognizes the possibility of sexual coercion in the lawyer-client relationship. The rules prohibit any sexual relationship between a lawyer and a client or representative of a client that "exploits or adversely affects the interests of the client or the lawyer-client relationship." Such relationships include, but are not limited to, ones "requiring or demanding sexual relations with a client or a representative of a client incident to or as a condition of a legal representation" and "employing coercion, intimidation, or undue influence in entering into sexual relations with a client or a representative of a client."[14] The use of "undue influence" is different from quid pro quo cases of sexual harassment. Professionals besides lawyers possess such influence and can use it to start sexual relationships with their clients or patients.

This disparity in power in professional relationships can be used by the professional to initiate relationships in ways other than through threats or coercive offers. The professionals we are discussing—as opposed, say, to plumbers—influence clients' and patients' decisions about matters at the core of their well-being, that is, their health and finances. The professional might try to use this influence in other areas of their clients' or patients' lives, such as their romantic or sexual relationships. The use of such "undue influence" might not fit our definition of coercion, because both parties might typically say to a third party, sincerely, that they *want* a sexual relationship with the other person. Such influence might not always be the cause for a patient or client entering into a sexual relationship with the professional. However, when it is the cause—and it can be difficult to determine this—it involves the use of non-physical power to compel another to act in a way that might not be in his or her best interest.

Some professionals can exert a power that is similar to *physical* power. The psychologist, for example, has the ability to influence the mental state of his patients. Although this power is, of course, limited and varies from psychologist to psychologist (as well as from patient to patient), it provides a more direct means than threats, offers, or undue influence to manipulate someone's behavior. The psychologist can use it to craft the impression the patient has of him, to manipulate the patient's beliefs about what would contribute to her psychological well-being, including what sorts of relationships she should form, and so on, all with the intention of initiating a sexual relationship with the patient.

Now, in ordinary cases of seduction the parties attempt to do the same. They say and do things to manipulate the impression the other person has of him or her. Most people do not have the same skills as a psychologist to do this, and they also might lack the psychologist's depth of knowledge of the other person and the sort of mental intimacy that is achieved in a therapeutic setting, both of which give the psychologist an advantage. Also, the conditions that send someone to a psychologist can make them more vulnerable to the latter's manipulations. However, there might be some who exceed the psychologist in charisma or charm, or who have other techniques for manipulating another's beliefs. We might characterize such a person as a modern-day *Don Juan* or *Doña Juana*. Yet when people apply these skills in ordinary interactions with others, it is typically not morally condemned. People can be subject to moral reprobation if they entirely fabricate the impression they give to another person, for example, by making up facts about their biography to make themselves more appealing. But in all social interactions, most people try to present to others the best sides of themselves and to conceal for as long as they can the less appealing aspects of their personalities or biographies.

An important difference between these ordinary cases and the professional relationship is the expectations of the parties in each situation. A patient enters a professional relationship with a therapist with expectations very unlike those of someone entering a social setting or, say, an internet dating service. The latter are expecting, if all goes well, to develop friendships or romantic/sexual relationships; the former typically do not have such expectations. While someone using an internet dating service should be skeptical to some extent of the information others present about themselves, the efficacy of the professional relationships we have discussed depends entirely upon trust. In its comment on the rule prohibiting sexual relationships, the Florida Bar draws attention to this: "The lawyer-client relationship is grounded on mutual trust. A sexual relationship that exploits that trust compromises the lawyer-client relationship." So persons entering a professional relationship typically will, and perhaps should, have more trust in the professional than they would for others in an ordinary social interaction. This makes them more susceptible to manipulation, including coercion, by the professional. Rules limiting or prohibiting sexual relationships in professional relationships are warranted by this fact, among others.

SEXUAL HARASSMENT IN PUBLIC

According to our core definition of sexual harassment, sexual harassment includes a disparity in power such that the victim of the harassment has less power than the harasser. According to my clarification of this condition earlier in this chapter, this power extends specifically over things that the victim values or desires. Such imbalances in power can be found in workplaces and in schools, and also in various professional relationships. But can they be found elsewhere?

In order to find cases of sexual harassment outside of workplaces and schools, we must look for actions that satisfy at least the core definition of sexual harassment. The cases to be considered below are alike in containing actions that are clearly sexual and unwelcome; most of the discussion will therefore be devoted to determining whether they satisfy the third condition of our core definition; that is, we will ask whether there is a power imbalance in these cases that is sufficient for sexual harassment. However, in the next and final section of this chapter, we will reconsider whether an imbalance in power is a necessary condition for sexual harassment.

Marriage has historically been a relationship of unequal power. The inequality can be caused by culture or economics, but more often by both. In many cultures, for example, the husband is regarded as the primary authority in marriage, and this authority has sometimes been considered exhaustive and absolute. In some countries, laws endorse this inequality by limiting women's rights of divorce; their ability to control dowries, inheritance, and other sources of income; and their rights of travel and habitation. Even in countries whose laws do not endorse these inequalities, society enforces some of them. A woman might defer to her husband's authority even though the law does not require it; she does so to avoid the condemnation of her peers, which can sometimes be more severe than legal condemnation. Also, in many countries economics can constrain the options of married women. On average and throughout the world, the earning power of men is greater than that of women. An inability to support herself financially might thus compel a woman to defer to her husband's authority and remain in a marriage that she would otherwise leave.

So, can a husband sexually harass his wife? For a long time, marital rape was considered a legal and moral impossibility. However, that is no longer the case. But what of the wife who has sex with her husband voluntarily, but only in order to avoid his divorcing her or curtailing her household allowance, since she has no sexual interest in him? This situation resembles quid pro quo harassment. Or, what of the wife who is repeatedly humiliated by her husband, in private and in front of others, by his derogatory remarks about her sexual attractiveness and desirability? This seems a lot like a hostile work environment. Let us suppose that the woman's options for leaving are limited. She will either be unable to support herself financially or will face legal or societal condemnation for doing so. These situations seem to meet the conditions of our core definition of sexual harassment. The actions directed toward these women are sexual and unwelcome, but they are endured in order to avoid the less desirable consequences of abandonment or other assertions of their husbands' power. So there exists an imbalance of power in these relationships such that the husband has power over things that are of value and importance to the woman. He uses that power to coerce his wife sexually. Women in these situations have very little power to change them, except by giving up things that are very valuable to them, which can even include their children.

But are there places outside the home in which a power similar to that exerted by husbands exists, such as in stores, parks, restaurants, bars, or—as in Marie's case—the sidewalk? If the men who are directing the catcalls and wolf whistles at Marie were her co-workers, their actions would constitute sexual harassment—specifically of the hostile work environment type—according to many legal definitions. The type of harassment that Marie endures is known as **stranger harassment** (sometimes also called "street harassment"). It is "unwanted sexual attention from strangers in public situations, such as on the street, public transportation, or in social establishments" (Wesselmann and Kelly, 452).[15] In addition to catcalls and wolf whistles, stranger harassment may involve verbal expressions of sexual interest, as well as demeaning sexual (or sexist) remarks; stares; all sorts of unwanted physical contact short of sexual assault, such as pinching or grabbing; and sexual gestures.

Like the same behaviors in a workplace, stranger harassment is offensive, sexist, and emotionally distressing, as well as simply rude. There is something wrong with the behavior directed at Marie by the men at the construction site, but is it sexual harassment? It is unwelcome and sexual, but there does not seem to be the disparity in power found in workplaces, schools, and many professional relationships. The construction workers do not have power over anything that is of central or great importance in Marie's life. Of course, as in many typical cases of sexual harassment, her dignity could be harmed, but she can avoid repeated injuries to her dignity by taking another route to work. We might then say that the construction workers have coerced her to walk three extra blocks to work. However, in taking another route to work, she is exhibiting a power that an employee and other victims of sexual harassment do not typically possess. She is inconvenienced, but a victim of sexual harassment in a school or workplace, for example, does not have the same power to avoid the harassment.[16] For the sake of such things as her job, academic career, finances, or health, she is coerced into enduring the sexual harassment. Of course she is free, in some metaphysical sense, to quit the job or leave the school, but in order to pursue those options she must give up something that is very valuable to her. The woman who walks an extra three blocks to get to work is not giving up nearly as much.

So, to apply the term sexual harassment to Marie's case might stretch the meaning of the term so far that it obscures important differences between her case and cases of sexual harassment in the workplace, schools, and professional relationships. Her case is different from these in not satisfying the third condition of our core definition. However, is that a necessary condition for sexual harassment? We will examine this question in the next section.

But first we should notice that we are considering Marie's experiences in isolation from the rest of her life, as well as the rest of the society to which she belongs. Imagine that Marie receives catcalls on her alternative route, as well is in the restaurants or stores she patronizes, the trains and buses she rides, and so on. Should we then say that she is a victim of sexual harassment? Such a situation is not entirely imaginary. A study of a group of college women found that 32 per cent experienced "catcalls, whistles, or stares" and 40 per cent "unwanted sexual attention" at least once a month; 31 per cent reported experiencing catcalls, etc., every few days. Also, 36 per cent of the women reported experiencing unwanted physical contact at least once a month (Fairchild and Rudman). An analysis of data from a much larger population, a national sample of Canadian women, found that 85 per cent reported some form of stranger harassment (more than their reports of non-stranger harassment, which was at 51 per cent).[17] These studies suggest that stranger harassment is a frequent and ubiquitous phenomenon.[18] If these forms of harassment are inescapable, as these statistics suggest, then their victims are like the victims of harassment in workplaces and schools. They are similarly powerless to resist or avoid the harassment. So the power asymmetry in these situations satisfies our core definition of sexual harassment.

This need not be the situation of every woman, in every society, who is the victim of stranger harassment. But even when the disparity in power condition is met, there might still be reasons for legally distinguishing between harassment on the street and in the workplace, as well as between the latter and harassment in marriage. With respect to the legal distinction, the law might not be the appropriate avenue for addressing stranger harassment; it certainly cannot be the exclusive avenue. Actions by groups other than the government that try to influence the beliefs and attitudes that are the source of stranger harassment, along with collective action to resist it, are more appropriate strategies for combating stranger harassment. Laws that ban the behaviors that constitute stranger harassment, such as catcalls, can conflict with laws protecting freedom of speech and assembly. In the Conclusion we will examine more fully the reasons for not extending sexual harassment law to include stranger harassment. With respect to marriage, the law simply cannot evacuate sex from marriage, although laws against domestic abuse can be strengthened and their enforcement can be improved. Ultimately, reductions of both forms of harassment will require changes that the law alone cannot effect, in particular, increasing the power of women in society. However, we will now consider whether the disparity in power condition even needs to be satisfied in order for sexual harassment to occur.

POWER AND SEXUAL HARASSMENT

Is disparity in power a necessary condition for sexual harassment? According to most legal definitions it is, although most of them are purposefully restricted to misuses of power in workplaces and schools (and not, for example, marriages). Some normative definitions of sexual harassment take it to be a necessary condition. Equality theories, for example, take sexual harassment to be a type of gender discrimination. MacKinnon writes, "Sexual harassment, most broadly defined, refers to the unwanted imposition of sexual requirements in the context of a relationship of unequal power" (MacKinnon, *Sexual Harassment*, 1). There must be some individuals with power to impose these requirements. Many dignity theories, however, do not take a disparity in power to be a necessary condition for sexual harassment. At least, their definitions do not explicitly state it as a condition.

Recall from Chapter Two Edmund Wall's definition of sexual harassment as a type of wrongful communication. In order for sexual harassment to occur, the harasser must repeat a message to the victim that he or she does not consent to receive. Wall's third condition for sexual harassment states, "Disregarding the absence of Y's consent,

X repeats a message of this form to Y" (Wall, "Sexual Harassment," 531). Neither this nor any of the other conditions refers directly to Y's or anyone else's power; however, it seems to be a causal condition for the fulfillment of Wall's third condition that Y be a *captive audience* to X's messages. That is, in order for X to repeat an unwelcomed message to Y, Y must not be able to walk away or otherwise avoid X's messages. This is the situation in workplaces and schools, where the targets of sexual harassment cannot easily escape the harassment.[19] They are compelled to stay for the sake of their income or education. We noted earlier the coercive element in hostile work environments; in these cases of sexual harassment, the power is typically not exerted by the harasser, but by the employers who are liable for the actions of their employees.[20] So, both of the normative definitions we have examined require disparity in power as a condition for sexual harassment.

I have already acknowledged the wrongness of similar actions performed outside a context of power, such as the actions of which Marie is a target as she walks by the construction site in the first version of her story we told. We considered briefly some reasons for legally distinguishing between workplace and stranger harassment, even when the disparity of power condition is met in cases of the latter, as in the second version of Marie's story that I told. However, there is at least one legal definition that does not draw such a distinction.

In 1998, Israel's legislature, the Knesset, passed the Prevention of Sexual Harassment Law (Kamir). The law prohibits sexual harassment in workplaces and all other social settings. It regards sexual harassment as resulting in both civil wrongs and criminal offenses. The law identifies and prohibits three sorts of sexual harassment. First, it prohibits behaviors that are already illegal according to Israel's Penal Law, such as sexual blackmail or indecent acts. The newer law grants victims the right to sue the harasser or employer. Second, it prohibits behaviors that are permitted when performed with mutual consent, such as sexual propositions and remarks about another's physical appearance or sexual desirability. When these remarks are made without the consent of their recipient, they constitute sexual harassment. The third category of sexually harassing behaviors identified by the law are those for which the consent or dissent of the target is irrelevant, such as a degrading or insulting remarks of a sexual nature. The law also recognizes that in cases of sexual messages, consent is also irrelevant when the recipient is a minor or "helpless person," a patient, an employee, or someone else who occupies a disadvantageous position in a power relationship.

So, according to Israeli law, the actions directed against Marie count as sexual harassment. If she worked in Tel Aviv, for example, she might have a case against the construction workers and perhaps their employer as well. In most other places, she would not have such legal redress. The law in Israel is much broader in scope than most other countries' laws on sexual harassment. However, Israeli law on sexual harassment might eventually influence legal definitions in other countries, such that other legal definitions become similarly expansive.

How does the legal definition in Israeli law affect our other definitions of sexual harassment? It need not have any effect on normative definitions. Both of the normative definitions we examined in Chapter Two required disparities in power; my amendment to those definitions does as well. The other behaviors that the Israeli law prohibits are still wrong, but they are wrong for different reasons. It would make things conceptually clearer if we had at least two different terms for these behaviors, i.e., "sexual harassment" and "stranger harassment." However, the Israeli law can influence descriptive definitions of sexual harassment, as it certainly will have done in Israel. MacKinnon explains the influence of the law on these definitions: "Legitimized and sanctioned, the legal concept of sexual harassment reenters the society to participate in shaping the social definitions of what may be resisted or complained about, said aloud, or even felt" (MacKinnon, *Sexual Harassment*, 57). In Israel, the common, everyday definition will probably cover cases like Marie's. Elsewhere, it appears that the descriptive definition of sexual harassment is coming to be used equally broadly, even though its legal definition—through which, as MacKinnon points out, it entered society—is restricted to harassment in the workplace.

SUMMARY

The power disparity that is present in workplace cases of sexual harassment can be found elsewhere. It exists in schools, as we examine closely in the next chapter. It also exists within professional relationships. The power that is exerted in all these contexts is different, but it can be used to coerce sexual favors from those with less power. This fact is one reason for normative prohibitions on sexual relationships between the parties in these relationships. However, one relationship which is partly constituted by sex—so it cannot be removed by the law—is marriage, and we have found that sexual harassment can occur between married partners; at least, certain behaviors within marriage meet the conditions of our core definition of sexual harassment.[21]

We have considered reasons for restricting the normative definition of sexual harassment to only actions that occur within situations containing an imbalance of power. We recognized that such imbalances can be found in cases of stranger harassment, and we considered one legal definition that does not make such imbalances a necessary condition of sexual harassment. Since the focus of this chapter has been on what behaviors outside of workplaces and schools satisfy our core definition of sexual harassment, I will wait until the Conclusion before fully examining the appropriateness of such laws.

REVIEW QUESTIONS

1. Summarize Nozick's definition of coercion.
2. What is the difference between threats and offers?
3. What constitutes a coercive offer?
4. What are some of the reasons why professional organizations prohibit sexual/romantic relationships between their members and their members' clients or patients?
5. What kind of power can professionals have over their clients/patients?
6. What is stranger harassment?

DISCUSSION QUESTIONS

1. If a lazy, incompetent employee is offered a promotion by her supervisor if she has sex with him, is she being coerced into having sex with him or in any other way harmed?

2. Should the codes of ethics governing professionals such as lawyers and physicians absolutely prohibit sexual relationships with clients or patients?

3. Can sexual harassment occur outside of the office or school? Try to think of cases (other than those discussed in this chapter) that meet at least our core definition of sexual harassment.

4. Can sexual harassment occur in marriage according to any of the legal or normative definitions we have examined so far?

5. If sexual harassment can occur in marriage, can a man ever be sexually harassed by his wife?

6. Do heterosexual relationships in a male-dominated society contain an element of coercion?

GROUP ACTIVITY

In small groups or individually, find the code of ethics for a professional organization on the local, state, or national level. Identify their policies on sexual harassment and related issues (e.g., sexual relationships with clients). In the full group, discuss the adequacy of these policies.

NOTES

1 <http://www.ama-assn.org/ama/pub/physician-resources/medical-ethics/code-medical-ethics/opinion814.shtml>; accessed 27 May 2010.

2 <http://www.apa.org/ethics/code/index.aspx>; accessed 27 May 2010.

3 <http://www.abanet.org/cpr/mrpc/rule_1_8.html>; accessed 27 May 2010.

4 <http://www.ladb.org/Publications/ropc.pdf>; accessed 4 Nov. 2011.

5 *New York Rules of Professional Conduct*, Rule 1.8j; <http://www.nysba.org>; accessed 13 Oct. 2011.

6 <http://www.lsuc.on.ca/WorkArea/DownloadAsset.aspx?id=2147485034>; accessed 4 Nov. 2011; the *Code of Professional Conduct* of the Nova Scotia Barrister's Society expresses similar concerns: <http://www.nsbs.org/documents/general/2011-09-19_CodeOfConductJan2012.pdf>; accessed 4 Nov. 2011.

7 Tracey Tyler, "Panel urges disbarment over sexual harassment," *Toronto Star* 6 July 2004: A02; Jeff Gray, "Lawyer gets new hearing," *The Globe and Mail* [Toronto] 17 March 2010: B8.

8 Carol Gentry and Stephen Nohlgren, "State accuses doctor of sex misconduct," *St. Petersburg Times* 5 June 1993: 1B; Sue Landry, "Embattled surgeon works in Bahamas," *St. Petersburg Times* 26 Aug. 1995: 1B. Several of his employees also won more than $20 million in sexual harassment lawsuits against him; see Mike Brassfield, "Plastic surgeon who lost license in trouble again," *St. Petersburg Times* 20 April 2002: 1B.

9 "Air Force Reprimands General for Numerous Sexual Affairs," *The New York Times* 23 Dec. 2004: late edition, A18.

10 A helpful discussion of coercion is found in Scott Anderson's *Stanford Encyclopedia of Philosophy* entry for coercion (see Appendix B).

11 We can threaten people in order to make them better off according to our perspective. For example, a parent can propose to his teenage son that he will take away his car if he doesn't stop getting speeding tickets. This is a threat even though the son would be better off without a car than driving recklessly. However, whether the person is coerced depends on whether *he* sees the situation as making him better or worse off. The teenage son would probably think that the proposal makes him worse off. So there can be benevolent coercions.

12 Threats like this are typically *implicit*. The supervisor does not need to state it; it is assumed by the employee. I will examine different sorts of implicit and explicit threats in the next chapter.

13 We will discuss in the next chapter how confident a recipient of such a proposal can be in the sincerity of the proposer's promise not to harm him or her if the proposal is refused. The recipient can have good reasons for doubting the sincerity of such a promise. In the present case, we will just assume that the recipient believes in its sincerity.

14 Rule 4-8.4 Misconduct; <http://www.floridabar.org>; accessed June 2, 2010.

15 See also Fairchild and Rudman.

16 Also, Marie is only inconvenienced temporarily, with respect to both the amount of time it takes each day to take this alternative route and the duration of the construction work.

17 Their analysis also revealed that "stranger harassment reduces feelings of safety while walking alone at night, using public transportation, walking alone in a parking garage, and while home alone at night" (Macmillan, Nierobisz, and Welsh, 319). The study of college women found their experiences with stranger harassment to be significantly related to self-objectification, for example feelings of shame (Fairchild and Rudman, 348).

18 The pervasiveness of stranger harassment is also well supported by other sorts of evidence: see, for example, Jennifer Lee, "Sex Offenses on the Subways are Widespread, City Officials are Told," *The New York Times* 20 Nov. 2009: A30; there is even a mobile phone application that allows victims of stranger harassment to post reports about incidents online: see

Karen Zraick, "Phone Apps Aim to Fight Harassment," *The New York Times* 8 Nov. 2010: A22.

19 This fact has led legal scholars, and the U.S. Supreme Court in *Robinson v. Jacksonville Shipyards, Inc.* (1991), to hold that punishing the speech that constitutes a hostile work environment is not an infringement on free speech rights, because the audience to the speech is effectively coerced into listening to it.

20 Some who deny that misuse of power is a necessary condition for sexual harassment fail to recognize this; see, e.g., Dodds et al.; Leeser and O'Donohue.

21 However, it does not seem that descriptive definitions of sexual harassment cover these behaviors yet.

CHAPTER 4

How Can Sexual Harassment Occur?

Sylvia is a graduate student currently working on her dissertation. She hopes to finish it in the next year and then receive her doctorate. She has been a graduate student for five years, and for the last two years she has been in a romantic and sexual relationship with her advisor, Daniel. They have kept their relationship a secret from their friends and colleagues because their university has a policy prohibiting romantic or sexual relationships between faculty and students. Daniel could face severe disciplinary action if the relationship were revealed, including termination. Sylvia also fears the opinions of her peers and other professors. She worries that the success she has enjoyed in graduate school will be attributed to her romantic relationship with a professor. For most of their relationship, both Sylvia and Daniel have been in love. However, Sylvia has recently lost interest in the relationship and is contemplating ending it. She is reluctant to do so, though, because she is afraid of Daniel's reaction.

The focus of this chapter is sexual harassment in schools. After a review of some laws and policies related to academic sexual harassment, I will focus on a specific kind of sexual harassment that can occur in schools: quid pro quo. More specifically, I will discuss often unrecognized ways under which this sort of sexual harassment can occur. The chapter's title is intended to express this focus. This chapter is an extension of the discussion in the previous chapter and, as such, much of it can be applied to sexual harassment in other contexts. Most of the examples, however, will be set in schools, principally higher education institutions.

In United States federal law, Title IX of the Education Amendments of 1972 prohibits sexual discrimination in educational institutions that receive federal funding. These include most private and public higher education institutions, public elementary and secondary schools, various technical schools whose students receive financial aid, and institutions that are not educational but contain educational programs that receive federal funds. Private schools that receive no federal funds are not covered by the law. Soon after courts recognized sexual harassment as discrimination under Title VII of the 1964 Civil Rights Act, they did the same for Title IX of the Education Amendments.

The law covers students of all ages and grades, and it protects them from sexual harassment by teachers, staff, and other students. Both types of sexual harassment are prohibited: quid pro quo and hostile environment. Title IX is enforced by the Office of Civil Rights of the U.S. Department of Education. Its policies define the two types of sexual harassment in this way:

> Quid pro quo harassment occurs when a school employee causes a student to believe that he or she must submit to unwelcome sexual conduct in order to participate in a school program or activity. It can also occur when an employee causes a student to believe that the employee will make an educational decision based on whether or not the student submits to unwelcome sexual conduct. For example, when a teacher threatens to fail a student unless the student agrees to date the teacher, it is quid pro quo harassment.

Hostile environment harassment occurs when unwelcome conduct of a sexual nature is so severe, persistent, or pervasive that it affects a student's ability to participate in or benefit from an education program or activity, or creates an intimidating, threatening or abusive educational environment. A hostile environment can be created by a school employee, another student, or even someone visiting the school, such as a student or employee from another school.[1]

Hostile environments in schools resemble those in workplaces. They can consist of degrading sexual remarks made by teachers or fellow students, the display of pornographic pictures, disparate treatment of female (or male) students by a teacher, and so on.[2] Quid pro quo cases are structurally similar, but the proposals that compel them cover different aspects of a person's life. It could be said that the power a teacher has over students is even more comprehensive—and therefore stronger—than that of a workplace supervisor. It covers students' grades, letters of recommendations, and other parts of their academic credentials, and all of these have an influence on their post-academic careers.

CONSENSUAL RELATIONSHIPS

Many universities have policies that either prohibit or discourage consensual sexual or romantic relationships between students and teachers or staff who have some authority over them. This, for example, is the policy at the University of Pennsylvania:

The relationship between teacher and student is central to the academic mission of the University. No non-academic or personal ties should be allowed to interfere with the integrity of the teacher-student relationship. Consensual sexual relations between teacher and student can adversely affect the academic enterprise, distorting judgments or appearing to do so in the minds of others, and providing incentives or disincentives for student-faculty contact that are equally inappropriate.

For these reasons, any sexual relations between a teacher and a student during the period of the teacher/student relationship are prohibited.... Teachers and academic supervisors who are sexually involved with students must decline to participate in any evaluative or supervisory academic activity with respect to those students.

The Provost, Deans, department chairs, and other administrators should respond to reports of prohibited sexual relations that are brought to them by inquiring further, and if such reports appear to be accurate, initiating appropriate disciplinary action or remedial measures against the teacher or supervisor involved.

... although this policy prohibits consensual sexual relations only between teacher/supervisor and that individual's student, the University strongly discourages any sexual relations between members of the faculty (or administration) and undergraduates.[3]

This policy prohibits consensual relationships between faculty and the students over whom they have some power, and it strongly discourages all other faculty-student relationships. Many other universities only discourage faculty-student relationships, but the trend is increasingly toward prohibiting them.

The reasons for prohibiting such relationships are similar to those we considered in the previous chapter for prohibiting relationships within professional relationships. As the University of Pennsylvania's policy explains, consensual sexual or romantic relationships can have deleterious effects on the efficacy of the teacher-student relationship, such as "distorting judgments or appearing to do so in the minds of others." They can also create "incentives or disincentives for student-faculty contact." The danger being flagged here seems to be quid pro quo sexual harassment. Despite the consensual nature of the relationship, the consent might only be apparent, and it could eventually turn from consent to coercion. In this chapter we will explore how this can happen.

Many companies have also adopted policies that prohibit consensual relationships between superiors and subordinates. Others strictly control these relationships, as well as ones between co-workers. The legal scholar Vicki Schultz laments this trend. She argues that sexual harassment law has been used by companies as an excuse for suppressing sexuality in the workplace, which, Schultz argues, is seen by many managers to be in conflict with organizational rationality. The purpose of eliminating sexual relationships from the workplace is not gender equality, but tighter control of employee behavior. She worries that efforts to banish sexuality from the workplace will actually exacerbate the problem of sexual harassment rather than alleviate it: "By displacing attention away from genuine problems of sex discrimination and associating feminism with a punitive stance toward sexuality, I believe the drive toward sexual sanitization may even undercut the goal of achieving gender equality" (Schultz, 2067). Schultz also worries about "threats to human intimacy" posed by these efforts at "sanitization" (2069). As noted at the start of Chapter Two, the workplace is increasingly becoming the primary arena of social interaction for most people. Policies prohibiting relationships between employees "deprive people of perhaps the single most promising avenue available for securing sexual partners" (Schultz, 2069). Schultz also worries that such policies will inhibit the development of friendships. The result, as Schultz sees it, is "a negative politics of sexuality as well as an improvised view of working life" (2070). We will consider these concerns later in the chapter.

LOVE AND PROHIBITED RELATIONSHIPS

Sylvia and Daniel are in a prohibited relationship. However, for at least most of their relationship they have been in love. Does that redeem their relationship? If they had respected their university's policy, they would have deprived themselves of a fulfilling relationship that was for both the source of much of their happiness, even if it is a relationship that eventually ends.

The topic of Plato's dialogue *Symposium* is love, and more specifically erotic love. One of the speakers in the dialogue, Pausanias,

observes that certain acts performed for the sake of love are toler-
ated more than if they were performed in pursuit of some other goal.
As he says, "The freedom given to the lover by both gods and men
according to our custom is immense" (183C). Such tolerance seems
evident today in how we permit and even encourage others to perform extraordinary acts, even humiliate themselves, in their pursuit
of love, but we are less tolerant when others act in this way in pursuit of other kinds of goal, for example, financial gain. Hence, we do
not have practices such as serenading loan officers or writing ballads
for prospective employers. For a lover, however, "No blame attaches
to [such] behavior: custom treats it as noble through and through"
(183B). Should we extend this tolerance to Sylvia and Daniel? That
is, should it be extended to relationships that are ordinarily morally,
and in some cases legally, prohibited? If the partners in such a relationship are in love with each other, should that excuse them from at least
moral, if not legal, sanction? The rest of the chapter will consider the
reasons for prohibiting consensual relationships. Among other things,
we want to know if there is anything wrong with Sylvia and Daniel's
relationship that cannot be mitigated by their love for each other.

TYPES OF THREAT

We discussed in Chapter Three how threats are a feature of many
quid pro quo cases of sexual harassment: they can be used to coerce
another person into a sexual relationship. In a discussion of sexual
harassment in schools, Nancy Tuana distinguishes five kinds of threat
that can figure in quid pro quo harassment:

   a) explicit intended threat, intention to harm
   b) explicit intended threat, no intention to harm
   c) implicit intended threat, intention to harm
   d) implicit intended threat, no intention to harm
   e) implicit unintended threat, no intention to harm. (Tuana,
      "Sexual Harassment in Academe," 56)

As I pointed out in the previous chapter, threats are effective only if made by someone whom the target of the threat believes has power to carry it out. The substance of the threat is a negative change to some aspect of the person's life or career over which the person making the threat has some power, for example, in academic cases, a student's grade. Tuana's list reveals the various ways in which a threat can be made.

An example of an *explicit* threat would be a professor saying to his or her student, "If you want to pass this class, you'll have to sleep with me." The professor need not intend the harm for his remark to be threatening, hence case (b).[4] It is sufficient that the student believes that harm will occur. *Implicit* threats are made when the person with power says or does something that requires the other to infer the threat. Here, too, there need not be an intention to harm. It is enough that the other believes that harm will occur for her to feel threatened and, subsequently, to be coerced into a sexual relationship.

The most interesting of these types of threat, or at least the one most relevant to our consideration of the case of Sylvia and Daniel, is (e): implicit unintended threat with no intention to harm. With such threats, its putative issuer intends neither to threaten nor to harm. Tuana's example of such a threat involves a college instructor and a student with whom she is interested in having a sexual relationship. The student visits the instructor during her office hours. The student has a "C" average in her class, but she believes that he is not working up to his potential. She proceeds to give him a "pep talk" that encourages him to work harder, but she warns him that she will fail him if he does not. The instructor's reason for this talk is only to encourage her student—whom she recognizes as bright from the comments he makes in class—to work up to his potential. Later that day, the instructor sees the student in a bar. She engages him in conversation and subsequently reveals that she is sexually attracted to him, with the intention of discovering whether her feelings are reciprocated. Upon her revelation, the student recalls his earlier conversation with the instructor and her warning about his failing performance in class. He takes his instructor's revelation not merely as an invitation to enter into a sexual relationship with her, but also as a *veiled* threat. He believes, given this context, that if he refuses her invitation then she'll fail him in her class. The instructor, however, has no such intention. Nevertheless, Tuana argues, the instructor's revelation of her sexual interest was negligent, since she should have known that her student might misconstrue her intentions and enter into a relationship out of a fear of retaliation; he would thus be coerced into the relationship:

> ... if a student has good reason to believe that he or she has been threatened by an instructor in order to procure sexual contact because of something that the instructor has said or done, then even if the instructor has not intended the threat, *the student has been harassed.* (Tuana, "Sexual Harassment in Academe," 55; italics in original)

Tuana says that having a "good reason to believe" that one is being implicitly threatened is a complex notion, but her story is intended to offer an example of a good reason. Even though the student's inference that his instructor is threatening him is false, it is still based on good reasons. These reasons consist of the instructor's revelation of her sexual interest in him in the context of his poor performance in her class and her earlier warning that she will fail him if he does not improve. Given the context in which her revelation was made, the student has good grounds for inferring that if he does not reciprocate the instructor's sexual interest, he will be harmed. Although Tuana does not say this, she would likely agree that the student need not be convinced—that is, certain—that he is being implicitly threatened; he might only have a suspicion that he is, but one strong enough to compel him to accept her invitation for a sexual relationship.

CONTEXT AND COERCION

In Chapter Three, we saw how coercion can occur in the absence of threats; in particular, we discussed coercive offers and how they can figure into quid pro quo cases of sexual harassment. In her essay

"Sexual Harassment: Offers and Coercion," Tuana identifies another way in which coercion can occur in the absence of a threat. The example she offers is meant to show how someone need not infer even an implicit threat, intended or not, in order to be harassed and coerced into a sexual relationship. The example involves a professor who does not merely reveal his sexual interest to a student, but also combines his revelation with an offer. She borrows this case from the philosopher Michael Bayles, with the purpose of criticizing his analysis of it. Specifically, the offer in question is made by a department chair to a mediocre graduate student of his department. The chair offers the student an assistantship, which she otherwise was not going to receive, in exchange for sleeping with him. The chair does not threaten to harm the student if she does not accept the offer, so the student, unlike the one in Tuana's previous example, does not infer an implicit threat. She accepts the offer and sleeps with him. Was she coerced into doing so?

This case is like the one introduced in the previous chapter about an unqualified employee who is offered a promotion in exchange for sex. I asked whether she was harmed in any way by her supervisor's offer. Bayles argues that in the student's case, she was not coerced, because even if she had had no interest in sleeping with the chair before the offer was made, doing so in fulfillment of an offer does not entail that she was coerced. Though she ends up doing something she would rather not do, she receives in exchange something she wants, an assistantship. As Bayles puts it, "the fact that a choice has an undesirable consequence does not make it against one's will" (Bayles, 143). He compares the situation to brushing one's teeth. Although we would rather have white teeth without the effort of brushing them, we are not coerced into brushing them. Bayles would be likely to say, therefore, that the employee who sleeps with her supervisor in exchange for a promotion is not coerced into doing so.

However, Tuana asks us to consider more thoroughly the context in which the chair's offer is made. She directs our attention to the power the chair has over not only assistantships, but also other aspects of the student's academic career. Tuana mentions the power the chair might have to assign members to her dissertation committee. He also might be the one to decide whether to give a departmental recommendation for jobs for which she is applying. In these and other ways, the chair has some potential influence over both her academic and post-academic careers. The student could recognize all of this and, in addition, make some inferences about the character of the chair based on his offer. As Tuana puts it, "the student now knows that the chairperson is the type of person who is willing to misuse his power to obtain what he wants, and thus has good reason to believe that this misuse of power might extend to penalizing a student who gets in the way of his wants" (Tuana, "Offers and Coercion," 34). In addition, the student probably understands, as we all do, that rejections of sexual invitations are ordinarily not lightly received; they are a wound to the ego. How such wounds are responded to, of course, varies from person to person. It is to be hoped that most of us would not actively attempt to inflict harm on the person who rejects us; the chair, however, has already revealed himself to the student as a person willing to use his power to get what he wants. Given this context, the student can reasonably (and likely) infer that the chairman might retaliate against her if she refuses his offer. Again, as in the previous example, the student need not be certain of this. A strong enough suspicion could be sufficient to compel her to accept his offer.

While the student has been neither explicitly nor implicitly threatened, the offer alone might coerce her into a relationship. If so, it is a type of coercive offer, but different from the kind of coercive offer considered in Chapter Three because it *does* involve a threat. The threat, however, is not made at the time of the offer; it is an anticipation of a threat that coerces the student. As Tuana explains, "the situation is one in which the threat of harm which the student fears is not made prior to or at the time of the offer, but will *come into existence* as a result of her refusal" ("Offers and Coercion," 35). A fear of future retaliation compels her to enter into a sexual relationship with the chairman. She does not want an assistantship so much that she will sleep with the chair in order to obtain one, but given the context in which the chair's offer was made, and her inference that harm could come to her later if she refused, she accepts his offer. The employee in our similar example from Chapter Three could have sex with her supervisor for analagous reasons and thus also be coerced into doing so.

It is reasonable and possible for anyone in the positions of the student and the employee in the examples above to make the same inferences; therefore, those with power should anticipate such inferences. Even if they have no intention to harm the other and are confident that no such intention would arise if their offer were refused, they should not make such offers. Tuana's analysis reveals that merely the context in which an offer is made can be coercive. She explains the benefit of her analysis: "the standard analysis of coercion is inadequate in that it omits sufficient reference to the context, the situation in which the action is performed" ("Offers and Coercion," 36). Offers in certain contexts can be coercive even without either explicit or implicit contemporaneous threats, and also without any prior alteration of the situation, as with Zimmerman's examples of coercive offers. This should, in theory at least, inhibit people in positions of power from making such offers.

RELATIONSHIPS BETWEEN FACULTY AND STUDENTS

The danger of coercion is one reason for prohibiting consensual romantic/sexual relationships between faculty and students. However, Sylvia and Daniel are already in a relationship, which neither was coerced into entering. Should their love for each other exempt them from at least any moral prohibition against such relationships? That is, there still might be reasons for them, or at least Daniel, to be subject to disciplinary action by the university. By failing to follow university policies they are likely doing something wrong: they are failing to follow the rules of the organization to which they belong, rules that other members of the organization are following. However, apart from this, are they doing anything else wrong? Also, did either do something wrong by entering the relationship?

The relationship could have started in at least a couple of different ways. First, Sylvia could have been sincerely and explicitly receptive to Daniel's expression of romantic/sexual interest in her. Second, Sylvia could have initiated the relationship and been the first to express her romantic/sexual interest in Daniel.

Are the efforts of a professor to initiate a romantic/sexual relationship with a student redeemed if the student expresses a reciprocal interest? The professor could always be mistaken about the sincerity of the student's interest. We have already seen that given the relationship of unequal power between them, the student could have reason to feign interest. Given that the student has strong reasons for concealing her true interests, the professor could not be confident enough in the sincerity of the other's expression of reciprocal interest to warrant entering the relationship and thus taking the chance that he is wrong. The harm that is risked—someone being coerced into a sexual relationship—is so great that it outweighs any possible benefits anticipated by either party when entering the relationship.

In relationships other than those in which there is a disparity of power, if one partner feigns reciprocal interest—because, say, she does not want to hurt the feelings of the other, or because she expects some benefit from the relationship, for example, financial—then the other partner has not done anything wrong by entering the relationship. It might make a difference if he knows that the other is only feigning a reciprocal interest but enters into the relationship anyway. If he conceals his knowledge of the other's true motivations from her, then he might be guilty of coercion. However, he is not obligated to investigate the motivations of the other beyond what he regards as her sincere expression of reciprocal interest. Where there is a disparity of power, however, the responsibilities of the person in power extend further. In fact, given the context in which his romantic/sexual interest is expressed, he cannot be sufficiently confident that the other's response to this interest will be sincere.

If a relationship were to develop, or even if a relationship of some sort already exists, the chances of mistaking the motivations of the other are less. But can the chances of being wrong about another's motivations ever be entirely relieved? It seems a feature of any relationship, romantic or other, that complete confidence in another's motivations and other mental states is not possible. We are often surprised by the actions of people we believe we know very well. For example, it is not uncommon to hear of people being surprised by a friend's revelation of a long-standing romantic interest in him or her, or by a partner's infidelity. Such surprises can occur at any point in a relationship's history. These surprises are possible because of our adeptness at concealing or feigning our mental states. Some of us are better at this than others, but we all possess this ability to some extent and we have all been victims of it.

What if the student initiates the relationship? That is, what if she expresses interest in a romantic/sexual relationship with the professor? We can first consider another sort of moral problem that such relationships might cause. We have discussed reasons for believing that a professor does something immoral by initiating a romantic/ sexual relationship with a student. Could the student be doing something wrong by attempting to intiate a relationship with his or her professor? Possibly, if she enjoys some academic benefits because of the relationship that her peers do not. A student will probably not, regardless of her performance, fail a class taught by her lover. Other academic benefits might accrue to her that are denied her peers. The receipt of such benefits can be a reason for both the student and the professor not to enter into a romantic relationship.

There are at least two other reasons why the professor should not enter into a romantic/sexual relationship with his or her student, even if the student initiates the relationship. First, although the professor has not coerced the student into entering the relationship, how confident can she be that she will not use her power to coerce the student to *remain* in the relationship? We have questioned the confidence we can have in our knowledge about others; we should be similarly skeptical about our knowledge of ourselves. Not only can another's actions surprise us, but we can sometimes be surprised by our own actions. Only experience, not introspection, can inform us of our rectitude. We come to conclusions about our character in the same ways others do—i.e., by observing current and past behavior. The philosopher Gilbert Ryle discusses this: "The way in which a person discovers his own long-term motives is the same as the way in which he discovers those of others"

(Ryle, 90). While we have a greater fund of experiences in our case than others in making this judgment—for example, our personal memories—our judgments about ourselves are also more susceptible to bias and can be less objective than the judgments of others. As Ryle explains, a person's "appreciations of his own inclinations are unlikely to be unbiased and he is not in a favourable position to compare his own actions and reactions with those of others. In general we think that an impartial and discerning spectator is a better judge of a person's prevailing motives, as well as of his habits, abilities and weaknessses, than is that person himself" (90). The professor is at least not entitled to complete confidence that she will not threaten or in some other way explicitly coerce the student to remain in the relationship.

But second, if the student eventually loses interest in the relationship and wants to leave it, we have seen that he or she can be coerced into remaining even if the professor does not explicitly or even intentionally threaten any harm. The student can infer such a threat on the basis solely of the other's power over her. That is, she can infer that the professor will use his power to retaliate against her. This could be one of the reasons why Sylvia is reluctant to end her relationship with Daniel. The fear of retaliation is not peculiar to relationships in which there is such an asymmetry in power. Retaliation by rejected lovers is common. However, for cases in which one partner holds power over the other, the harm that can result from retaliation is potentially much greater. It can be wielded over aspects of the other partner's academic or professional career, and thus their livelihood, their standing within their profession, and so on.

I have presented two sets of reasons for believing that relationships like Sylvia and Daniel's are morally problematic. It is not made less so by the facts that it began with both of them being sincerely interested in pursuing it and that during most of it they were in love. This is because, first, the confidence that Daniel can have in the veracity of Sylvia's expression of reciprocal interest could not have been strong enough to warrant risking the harm if he was wrong, and, second, he could not be confident enough that he will not harm her in the future or that she will not otherwise be coerced into remaining in the relationship. In cases in which the partners are not in love, and so have less knowledge of each other, these reasons are even stronger against their entering into a relationship with each other when a disparity in power exists between them.

However, the two ways in which we imagined Sylvia and Daniel's relationship developing is perhaps not realistic. A third, more likely, possibility is that it slowly dawned upon each of them that their romantic/sexual interests were reciprocated. So it was not a matter of Sylvia's or Daniel's one day announcing their interest. Rather, soon after both realized their reciprocal romantic interests, the relationship began. If this were the case, Daniel should be entitled to greater confidence in Sylvia's expression of reciprocal interest. However, the second danger is not alleviated. As she has been described, Sylvia is inhibited from ending the relationship because of her fear of Daniel's reaction. She could reasonably fear retaliation and thus be coerced into remaining in the relationship.[5]

Should the moral prohibition against sexual/romantic relationships between professors and students be translated into policy? For example, should universities adopt a policy, like the one at the University of Pennsylvania, which absolutely prohibits such relationships? It can be argued that this policy limits the freedom of both professors and students to enter relationships of their choosing. Some have argued that these policies are paternalistic in their application to students; they assume that students are incapable of deciding on what relationships to enter. For female students, this paternalism tends to reflect the patriarchal view that women lack the ability to make decisions about their own well-being.[6] While the policies are intended to protect women (who are more often the victims of sexual harassment), they tend to promote the very conditions that make them victims of sexual harassment. There are also worries, such as those of Vicki Schultz, that policies regulating the sexual and/or romantic relationships in workplaces and schools are "threats to human intimacy" (Schultz, 2067). Schultz also argues that sexuality is ineradicable, and that policies that attempt to "sanitize" it from workplaces or schools will only result in increased "surveillance and discipline," and not less sexuality (2068).

One possible response to these concerns by a defender of a policy like the one at the University of Pennsylvania is to point out this option for potential couples in the prohibited relationships: they can wait for the academic relationship to end before beginning the romantic/sexual relationship. For example, Daniel and Sylvia could wait until she graduates, or he could stop being her dissertation advisor. They will still have to make a sacrifice in order to conform to the policy: the time they would have spent together either in the prohibited relationship or in another valuable relationship, the academic one; still, as a defender of the policy could argue, the policy is not preventing them from forming a relationship. However, in the workplace there is typically not the same flexibility to enter and leave relationships; greater sacrifices, such as quitting a job or position, would be required to satisfy the policy.[7] All of these worries about policies regulating romantic and/or sexual relationships can lead one to oppose their implementation while still supporting the moral prohibition against such relationships; this position would regard employers and university administrators as inappropriate enforcers of the moral prohibition. It might simply not be the business of these organizations to regulate the romantic/sexual relationships of their members. The members themselves—employees, students, faculty, and so on—must be the sole enforcers of moral rules covering such relationships.

SELF-ASSESSMENTS AND THE JUDGMENTS OF OTHERS

Among the reasons for the moral prohibition on relationships between professors and students (as well as employers and employees), there is one that has nothing to do with the threat of coercion.

How, and what, we think of ourselves often depends on the judgments of others. Their admiration or disapprobation can figure into our self-assessments. As such, these judgments can contribute to, or detract from, our self-image. Whether or not they should is another matter, but there is no denying that, for all of us, what others think of us contributes in some degree to how we think of ourselves. We can use the judgments of others, either through how they contribute to our self-image or more directly, when making certain decisions. This is especially true of the judgments made about us by our teachers and employers, at least with respect to some of the most important decisions we make. Their judgments can figure into decisions about whether or not to go to graduate school, to seek a raise or a promotion, to start a new career, to use our talents to start our own business, and so on. These decisions are among those that can have the most profound and long-lasting effects on our lives. But also, apart from these kinds of decisions, our self-image is important to us. Our happiness depends a great deal on how we think of ourselves.

However, when these judgments are combined with seduction, their veracity becomes suspect. Every seduction involves flattery, and flattery involves making judgments that are not necessarily false but are exclusively positive and made with less attention to their veracity than is ordinary. Yet the seducer might not even be aware of his flattery. Stendhal, for example, believed that every lover is subject to the phenomenon he called "crystallization," in which every fault of the beloved is obscured, and any virtue he can think of is attributed to the beloved. In Plato's dialogue *Phaedrus*, the speaker Lysias advises us not to trust the praises of lovers, because "their judgment is weakened by their passion" (233b). Both express the idea that romantic or sexual desire makes one's judgments less objective; they do not proceed from investigation or any other similar rational process but are motivated mostly by desire and emotion.[8]

While it might also be true that the attention of a lover can better discern the virtues of his beloved, apart from some independent verification of his judgments, two things might result for the beloved. Believing that the judgments of a lover should be suspect, she might, first, distrust their sincerity and hence be less confident to make decisions based upon them, even though they might be true. Or she might simply decide not to include them in her self-assessments and thus possibly deprive herself of their possible contribution to her happiness. Or, if she is not suspicious of their veracity, she might make important decisions based on false, or otherwise less than true, judgments about her.

For example, a teacher might make what is a sincere and accurate judgment about his student's talents, but if this judgment is combined with, or precedes, an attempt to initiate a romantic relationship with her, the student, even if receptive to the idea of a relationship, might still become suspicious about the veracity of her instructor's judgments. She is then deprived of an accurate way to assess her talents, something she is paying for or in some other way owed. Similarly, an employee might be reluctant to make career decisions based on the judgments of her boss after his romantic affections are revealed to her. Also, if these suspicions do not arise, and the judgments are false, the student or employee might make decisions based on inaccurate judgments of her abilities or talents, which could result in her being harmed in some way.

Teachers have an obligation to be as honest and open with their students as possible. While they might not always be welcome, a student should be able to get from the teacher accurate reports about her skills and talents. While employers do not have the same kind of obligation to their employees, they should know that their employees might use their opinions in order to make important decisions. These considerations make not only an attempt to initiate a romantic relationship morally problematic, but also merely the expression of romantic or sexual interest.

SUMMARY

Students can be subjected to hostile environments created by their teachers or their peers. They can also be coerced into sexual relationships with their professors and other authorities in their school. This chapter has revealed the various ways in which coercion can occur. Coercive threats can be either explicit or implicit, and in either case no harm might be intended. The target of the threat can infer the intention, in addition to the threat itself. The inference might be based solely on the context in which the proposal of a sexual relationship is made. Coercion can also occur in anticipation of a threat. So the target of the proposal might believe that it contains neither a threat nor an intention to harm but accepts the proposal solely to avoid an anticipated emergence of a threat.

This discussion of possible threats has presented strong reasons against relationships in which a disparity in power exists between the partners, for example, professor-student relationships. However, any conclusion in favor of an absolute prohibition of such relationships in workplaces or on campuses has been avoided. Readers should try to decide whether or not there should be one.

REVIEW QUESTIONS

1. What are the five different ways in which a threat can be made, according to Nancy Tuana?
2. What are some of Vicki Schultz's complaints against regulation of employee relationships?
3. What are some reasons for regulating relationships between professors and students?
4. How, according to Tuana, can certain contexts make offers coercive?

DISCUSSION QUESTIONS

1. Do you share Vicki Schultz's worries about the "sexual sanitization" of the workplace? Can the same worries be applied to schools?
2. Should universities have a policy that absolutely prohibits romantic or sexual relationships between professors and students?
3. Do you agree with Tuana that context alone can sometimes make an offer coercive? Can greater knowledge about the person making the offer eliminate its coerciveness?
4. Is there anything wrong with Sylvia and Daniel's relationship? If so, should they end it?
5. Can students sexually harass professors (or employees their supervisors)? Do they hold any sort of power that would make them capable of coercion?

GROUP ACTIVITIES

1. Working in large or small groups, come up with examples of threats for each of the five kinds of threat identified by Tuana. Do

this for each of the following three contexts in which threats can occur: school, workplace, and professional relationships.

2. Find your school's sexual harassment policy. Discuss answers to these questions: (a) Does it provide sufficient protections to the victims of sexual harassment, as well as those accused of sexual harassment? (b) Are the procedures for reporting cases of sexual harassment clear and in other ways adequate (e.g., do they contain sufficient protections for confidentiality)? (c) Can it help reduce cases of sexual harassment?

NOTES

1 <http://www2.ed.gov/about/offices/list/ocr/qa-sexharass.html>; accessed 5 July 2010

2 In spring 2011, the U.S. Department of Education's Office for Civil Rights began investigating a complaint by students of a sexually hostile environment at Yale University. Incidents cited in the complaint included fraternity pledges parading past residence halls shouting "No means yes!" and a widely distributed e-mail—titled a "preseason scouting report"—in which male students evaluated the sexual desirability of incoming female freshmen. The complaint also accuses the university of inadequately dealing with incidents of sexual assault. See Lisa W. Foderaro, "At Yale, Sharper Look at Treatment of Women," *The New York Times* 8 April 2011: A22.

3 <http://www.upenn.edu/affirm-action/shisnot.html>; accessed 5 July 2010.

4 Explicit threats need not be verbal (Nozick, 444). An example of a non-verbal explicit threat is a professor who invites his student to have a sexual relationship with him and, when she hesitates, he picks up a test of hers and simulates with his finger or a pencil changing the grade on it from an "A" to an "F."

5 I have been assuming that the professor holds all the power and the student none. However, can a student ever hold sufficient power to coerce a professor (or an employee her supervisor)? A discussion question of this chapter invites readers to reflect on this matter.

6 Jane Gallop offers such an argument, as well as a defense of sexual relationships between professors and students, in her book *Feminist Accused of Sexual Harassment*.

7 Schultz discusses "love contracts" as a means for avoiding absolute prohibitions on workplace romances (Schultz, 2126–29). These are legal forms signed by the parties of a workplace relationship that documents their consent in entering the relationship. According to what has been discussed in this section, "love contracts" cannot be an effective means of documenting consent. A party can be coerced into signing the contract, and it does not eliminate the possibility of future coercion.

8 For some scientific evidence in support of this claim, see Murray, Holmes, and Griffin.

Conclusion: How Do We Prevent Sexual Harassment? Five Recommendations

Sexual harassment in workplaces and schools is likely to remain a problem for some time to come. Changes to the law, such as the United States Supreme Court recognition of sexual harassment as a form of sex discrimination in 1986, are a first step to combating sexual harassment. However, the law does not provide a complete response to sexual harassment. As we saw in previous chapters, the law in many countries does not cover behaviors that many would consider sexual harassment. Also, while the law can discourage sexual harassment, it cannot address the emotions and beliefs that motivate it.

This final chapter draws on conclusions reached in previous ones in order to make some specific recommendations about how to prevent sexual harassment. These recommendations include actions that societies can take, such as changing the law, as well as actions that individuals can take to address the emotions and beliefs that are behind the occurrences of sexual harassment. Throughout the chapter, I recommend that we appreciate the seriousness of sexual harassment as a harm to both individuals and society, acquire and promote an understanding of sexual harassment, and acknowledge all of its possible causes, including failures in mutual understanding. I also recommend ways for workplaces and other organizations to implement initiatives that combat sexual harassment.

1. UNDERSTAND SEXUAL HARASSMENT

One of the objectives of this book has been to increase readers' understanding of sexual harassment, which can ultimately help in its prevention. We cannot effectively prevent something if we do not understand it; our efforts will be misdirected by focusing either on the wrong thing or not enough on the right thing.

There are at least three components to a complete and accurate understanding of sexual harassment. First of all, there is the *meaning* of sexual harassment. We saw in Chapter One that the definition of sexual harassment remains unsettled; however, attention to the various ways in which it has been defined is necessary for arriving at our own definitions. It will also cause us to be more reflective about the nature of sexual harassment and thus more deliberate in our identifications of cases of sexual harassment. We will rely less on presumed understandings or apparently intuitive grasps of the concept.

We also saw that, most generally, there are at least three different kinds of definition of sexual harassment: descriptive, legal, and normative. A *descriptive* definition reflects how people use the term in ordinary discourse. *Legal* definitions are established by courts and legislatures. They arise from, but subsequently influence, descriptive definitions of sexual harassment. A *normative* definition tells us what is wrong with sexual harassment. This is the second component of an understanding of sexual harassment, and the strongest motivation for acting to prevent it. As discussed in Chapter Two, there have been two influential approaches to explaining the wrongness of sexual harassment. There are *dignity* theories, which see the harm of sexual harassment to be primarily against the dignity of the victim. *Equality* theories, on the other hand, view the harm of sexual harassment to be primarily discrimination. It is a group harm that affects all the members of the group to which the victim belongs, not just individual victims. I identified problems with both approaches and, instead of deciding between them, recommended that both be regarded as identifying some of the harms caused by sexual harassment. I expanded on these approaches by identifying a further harm that sexual harassment causes, particularly to at-will employees: it leaves them uncompensated for the extra work they perform in order to receive various job-related benefits and to maintain their employment.

Finally, as the title of this chapter suggests, we should understand how to prevent sexual harassment. Our knowledge of what sexual harassment is and what is wrong with it will help inform strategies to prevent it. In addition to this knowledge about the concept of sexual harassment, which has been the focus of this book, familiarity with research in the social sciences is also required to formulate strategies for preventing it. Some research of this sort is shared in the next section, but further research must be drawn upon, including research on the victims of sexual harassment, the organizational conditions that contribute to its occurrences, as well as the characteristics of the typical harasser. Fortunately, a good deal of this research is currently taking place. It is up to those who have the power to implement this research to take it into account.

2. DEVELOP AND IMPLEMENT SEXUAL HARASSMENT INITIATIVES

Almost all sexual harassment laws cover only the harassment that occurs in workplaces, schools, and similar organizations. Most normative definitions and our own core definition of sexual harassment require a disparity in power between the harasser and victim. Such disparities are found in hierarchical organizations such as the ones mentioned. These organizations are responsible for the sexual harassment that occurs within them; they can be held legally, socially, and morally responsible for it. This puts them on the front lines, so to speak, of the battle against sexual harassment. In order to reduce incidents of sexual harassment—as well as their liability for incidents that do occur—organizations should take initiatives to combat sexual harassment.

Barbara Gutek distinguishes three components of an organizational initiative on sexual harassment: policies, procedures, and training. These are steps that organizations have found most useful for preventing sexual harassment and protecting themselves against lawsuits (Gutek, 187). The policy is a text disseminated to all the members of the organization, stating that the organization does not condone and will not tolerate sexual harassment.[1] It should include all the relevant legal definitions of sexual harassment. For example, businesses in the United States should include the EEOC definition in their policy; since schools have both employees and students, they should include the EEOC definition along with the U.S. Department of Education's definition (Appendix A). Any applicable local definitions should also be included. In order to contend with a possible multiplicity of definitions, the policy should state that behaviors that meet any of these definitions will be considered sexual harassment. To facilitate understanding of these definitions, the policy should include examples of sexual harassment or categories of behaviors that could constitute sexual harassment (Gutek, 189).

In order for it to be an effective policy, it must be known by all the members of the organization. It cannot be buried in an employee or faculty manual that no one ever reads. Therefore, the entire policy should be easily accessible. A link to an electronic copy of it from the company's website is essential. Also, a summary of the policy should be posted on bulletin boards that contain other information frequently read by employees. Organizations should also actively disseminate the policy. It can be distributed through e-mail periodically, included in new employee packages, and reproduced in company newsletters. A university can publish its policy periodically in the university's newspaper and include it in new-student orientation sessions.

The text that contains the policy should also include an explanation of the procedures for handling reports of sexual harassment. This should include, most importantly, information on how victims can report incidents of sexual harassment. This information should be prominently displayed in the versions of the policy distributed among the organization's members. It should advise victims on the best ways to prepare a report, for example, taking detailed notes about the incidents, gathering witnesses, and so on. The procedures should provide victims with a list of people who can receive their reports. This should not be limited to immediate supervisors, since these are many of the harassers (Gutek, 191). Those who make reports should also be made aware of how these reports will be handled.

Organizations have a choice on whether to have formal or informal procedures for handling complaints. Each approach has benefits and drawbacks. A formal procedure would require that the accusor submit a signed complaint, which would be investigated by someone who could be presumed to be impartial. Following the investigation, either this person or a committee to whom he or she reports would make a decision on the complaint. If it were found that sexual harassment has occurred, then sanctions against the harasser or other remedies would be ordered. There should be an appeals process for both the accuser and accused.

Formal procedures should also include mechanisms for maintaining the confidentiality of both the alleged victim and harasser. Without these mechanisms, victims of sexual harassment will be reluctant to report the harassment. However, Gutek advises against promising anonymity to those who make complaints:

> Once the alleged harasser is confronted with the information
> that someone has lodged a complaint, he or she can often guess
> correctly who made the complaint. If it is not possible to guarantee
> anonymity, then it makes no sense to promise it. It can also cause
> additional anguish for the complainant, who is probably suffering
> enough already. (Gutek, 190)

Alleged harassers need protections as well. Even charges proven to be false can damage someone's reputation and cause other distress. While there are criminal and civil penalties for bringing false charges in a court of law, workplaces should not try to replicate such penalties or in other ways try to discourage the bringing of charges, because such actions might inhibit people from making genuine complaints. Targets of false accusations retain the right to sue persons who make them, and employers can fire those who make malicious false accusations against fellow employees. However, such penalties should not be formalized as a part of the organization's sexual harassment procedures.

Formal procedures require victims to file a formal complaint and participate in a formal investigation of their charges. Victims can reasonably be intimidated by this process: they might regard it as a fight between them and a more powerful organization, and so might consider their chances of "winning" to be slim. Even if they overcome their reluctance to participate in such a "fight," joining it can cause stress that is in addition to that caused by the harassment. Also, many victims simply want the harassment to stop; not only do they not desire a battle over it, but they also do not want the harasser to be punished. As Gutek puts it, "Formal methods, in a sense, provide more than they want—or something other than they want" (Gutek, 192).

Informal procedures, on the other hand, do not include specific steps for the handling of sexual harassment complaints. An informal procedure, in contrast to a typical formal procedure, will not result in a clear winner or loser. Its aim is mostly to stop the harassment. It will not be as public as a formal procedure, which better ensures the confidentiality of the complainant and alleged harasser. However, this may lead victims to believe that they are the only ones being harassed,[2] which may discourage them from bringing a complaint (Gutek, 192). Another disadvantage of an informal procedure is the greater likelihood of a "slipshod job" (193). This can fail to eliminate the harassment and could pose problems for the organization if a lawsuit is brought.

Organizations may indeed have both formal and informal procedures; victims can be allowed to choose which set of procedures to use. Gutek recommends that victims also be informed of alternatives to the company's formal or informal procedures for handling complaints: "because most targets of sexual harassment never report sexual harassment, organizations should supplement their own formal and/or informal procedures with suggestions for how targets can try to handle sexual harassment on their own" (191).[3] These suggestions can include recommendations of reading materials that explain such self-help. The company's procedures should not be the only avenue that victims have for addressing sexual harassment.

Policies and procedures should take seriously the concerns of Vicki Schultz and others about the "sanitized workplace." As discussed in Chapter Four, policies that prohibit sexual relationships between employees or in other ways limit employees' sexual expression might offer some legal protection to the organization, but they do not necessarily protect its members from sexual harassment. Schultz argues that they might even increase cases of sexual harassment by "displacing attention away from genuine problems of sex discrimination and associating feminism with a punitive stance toward sexuality" (Schultz, 2067). However, the remedies that would allow us to entirely abandon sexual harassment policies and procedures require the success of actions beyond the workplace. Indeed, as Schultz acknowledges, these remedies will fall outside of legal reform (2163). In particular, achieving gender equality and reforming attitudes toward sexuality in society more broadly will reduce sexual harassment more than will workplace initiatives or changes in the law. Nevertheless, until those changes are made, the law and workplace policies are necessary for reducing sexual harassment.

Training is the final step organizations can take toward addressing and reducing sexual harassment. It is another way in which the organization's policy and procedures can be disseminated to its members. Training can also make the organization's members better able to identify sexual harassment; this can cause some to modify their behavior or influence that of others. A study with college students showed positive correlations between sexual harassment training and the trainees' perceptions of sexual harassment and their ability to identify correctly incidents of sexual harassment (Moyer and Nath). In another study, researchers found that sexual harassment training is associated with a greater probability of a trainee "considering unwanted sexual gestures, remarks, touching, and pressure for dates to be a form of sexual harassment" (Antecol and Cobb-Clark).[4]

The participants in training may include supervisors or all the members of the organization. The goals of the training and sometimes legal matters will determine who should participate, as well as whether the training is voluntary. I discuss below how certain laws mandate sexual harassment training for certain employees and how some organizations institute training to indemnify themselves from lawsuits. The content of the training should include the relevant legal definitions of sexual harassment, the organization's policy and procedures on sexual harassment, and other information relevant to identifying and reporting incidents of sexual harassment. The training may also aim to sensitize employees to sexual harassment.

The training materials may be developed in-house or obtained from some outside source.[5] Training methods can be passive or active, or a combination of both. Passive methods involve delivering information through presentations, videos, online tutorials, and so on. Active methods can involve role-playing, interactive discussions, and individual or group exercises on passively presented material. Passive methods might be most effective when the goal is to equip trainees with particular knowledge (for example, the legal definition of sexual harassment, the organization's policy and procedures, and so on). If, instead, the goal is to change the attitudes and behaviors of trainees, then active methods are often more successful (Sogunro). Post-training activities can help reinforce this training. These can include refresher courses or simply distributing materials to trainees for later consultation; they can also include assessing their knowledge and application of training in performance reviews or in other ways that reward the retention of the training. Indeed, one study has found post-training activities to be correlated with a lower number of sexual harassment complaints (Perry et al.).

Despite the studies that have been mentioned, there remains a paucity of research on the effectiveness of sexual harassment training. It also appears that the results of research are not always being implemented in actual training. A recent study found gaps between this research and what is recommended in the literature read by those who implement sexual training; these gaps include the latter making recommendations that are not supported by and sometimes even inconsistent with the research, as well as the latter being silent on findings in the research on the most effective training methods (Perry, Kulik and Field). The results of this study raise the concern that despite the increasing prevalence of anti-harassment training in organizations, much of the training might be ineffective. However, organizations have other reasons for training besides informing and changing the behavior of trainees. Legal concerns are an important motivation behind implementing sexual harassment training.

In the United States, no federal law mandates sexual harassment training in workplaces or schools. However, many states require training of supervisors and/or employees in government offices, and four states—California, Connecticut, Maine, and New Jersey—require businesses with a certain minimum number of employees to provide sexual harassment training to supervisors (Martucci and Lu).[6] Where sexual harassment training is not mandated, it still provides some legal protection to organizations. It can "serve a symbolic purpose" by indicating to courts that they take sexual harassment seriously; this can reduce their liability in sexual harassment cases (Perry et al., 191). While it might serve such purposes, one study has found that when legal compliance is the primary reason for implementing training, the use of "best practices" in training has no effect on the success of the training (Perry et al.). When training is meant primarily to serve a "symbolic purpose," the other possible goals of training, such as reducing incidents of sexual harassment, are less likely to be met.[7]

I have focused in this section on sexual harassment initiatives in organizations such as schools and workplaces. Professional organizations would also benefit from adopting initiatives that go beyond merely prohibiting sexual harassment in their codes of ethics. These initiatives would be aimed at protecting both the professionals and their clients and colleagues. For example, professional organizations can offer sexual harassment training to their members. This would sensitize members to sexual harassment and inform victims of the available remedies within the organization or through the courts. Some organizations can punish or take other remedial action against members that commit sexual harassment. For example, bar associations, in conjunction with the courts, have the power to take away a member's license to practice law.

3. ADVOCATE FOR CHANGES IN THE LAW

Working collectively, the citizens of a democracy can influence their nation's laws. Over the course of this book I have identified several problems with the approaches taken by legal systems to address sexual harassment. For example, we learned in Chapter Two that United States law is unable to protect victims of equal-opportunity harassment. It also has related difficulties protecting victims of harassment based on sexual orientation. These limitations are due to the basis of sexual harassment law in anti-discrimination law, in particular Title VII of the Civil Rights Act of 1964. Title VII recognizes only five protected classes: race, color, religion, sex, and national origin. Not until 1986 did the United States Supreme Court recognize sexual harassment as a form of sex discrimination. The victims of equal opportunity harassment and harassment based on sexual orientation, along with their advocates, wait for the court to extend Title VII to cover their cases. As discussed in Chapter Two, the Supreme Court in *Oncale v. Sundowner Offshore Services, Inc.* (1998) acknowledged the possibility of same-sex sexual harassment. However, the implications of this ruling remain unclear. The legal scholar Andrea Meryl Kirshenbaum has reviewed most of the lower court rulings subsequent to *Oncale* and has concluded that understanding of the "because of ... sex" requirement of Title VII, in particular, has become more muddled: "there is a consensus about the 'because of ... sex' requirement, and that consensus is that no court truly knows what it means" (Kirshenbaum, 173).

Rosa Ehrenreich proposes an alternative to Title VII for addressing workplace harassment. She laments the exclusive focus on Title VII and notes the "doctrinal somersaults" that scholars must go through to get all forms of sexual harassment—for example, same-sex sexual harassment—regarded as discrimination (Ehrenreich, 3).

She calls for a more "pluralistic understanding of workplace harass-ment" that would provide legal remedies to all victims of workplace harassment, regardless of their gender or sexual orientation (4). She outlines an approach that uses common-law tort causes of action to address workplace harassment.[8] While she believes Title VII would still play an important role, especially for women who are victims of discrimination, her approach would provide a legal remedy for other victims of harassment that would not require new interpretations of Title VII or legislation.

Another change to the law considered in this book was related to the at-will doctrine. I presented Lea Vander Velde's view that the at-will doctrine contributes to sexual harassment and other forms of discrimination by limiting the power of employees, and concluded that relaxing the doctrine further or abandoning it in favor of a just cause doctrine should increase the ability of employees to resist sexual harassment. Most industrialized nations follow the just cause doctrine. The United States is an exception; while the at-will doctrine has been relaxed over the years, it is unlikely to be replaced as a foundation of employment law for some time to come.

Enacting changes like these to the law requires either new legisla-tion or changes in how courts interpret existing law. The Employment Non-Discrimination Act, a proposed bill currently stalled in the U.S. Congress, is an example of the former approach. It would prohibit dis-crimination on the basis of sexual orientation and gender identity. It is difficult for ordinary citizens to advocate for changes in how courts interpret the law. While legal scholars can have some influence through their writings on judicial decision making, citizens have a more indi-rect influence through their election of representatives who appoint and confirm federal judges.[9] Protests and demonstrations, or more subtle forms of expression, such as letter writing, are likely to have little direct influence on judicial decision making but may eventually influence the views of politicians and the general public. Ultimately, in a reasonably well-working democracy, the views of scholars and all other citizens should have an influence on the law as it comes out of both the legislatures and courts.

Among the more sweeping changes to the law that have been considered are ones that would expand not only the pool of potential victims of sexual harassment, but also the types of place in which sexual harassment could occur. In the United States, Title VII of the Civil Rights Act and Title IX of the 1972 Education Act Amendments prohibit sexual harassment in most workplaces and schools, respectively. In Chapter Three we examined the law in Israel that bans sexual harassment in all social arenas, not just within organizations. Other changes to the law can also address the so-called stranger harassment that was discussed in Chapter Three. However, laws guaranteeing freedom of expression pose an obstacle to such expansions to the law. The case of pornography can help illustrate this problem.

In addition to being a strong and influential advocate of sexual harassment law, Catharine MacKinnon has been an important proponent of laws to combat pornography. In the 1980s, MacKinnon and Andrea Dworkin helped draft ordinances in Minneapolis and Indianapolis that would have made pornography a violation of civil rights, allowing those who have been harmed by it to pursue civil remedies against its producers and distributors.[10] Similar ordinances were drafted in Cambridge, Massachusetts, and Bellingham, Washington. They were all either voted down or eventually found unconstitutional by the U.S. Supreme Court. However, some of the reasoning behind these ordinances was adopted by the Supreme Court of Canada in *R. v. Butler* (1992).[11]

MacKinnon and Dworkin do not argue that pornography should be denied First Amendment protections because it violates community standards of decency, is obscene, or is in some other way inherently immoral. Instead, they employ the same strategy that was used against sexual harassment. They argue that pornography is a form of discrimination. In particular, through its production and dissemination, pornography discriminates against women by contributing to their subordination.

MacKinnon and Dworkin contend that many women have been coerced into appearing in pornographic films; women who have not been coerced are still exploited by its producers through low pay and other forms of mistreatment. These claims have been contested by many women who insist that they have freely chosen to participate in pornography and that it is paternalistic of others to claim their participation is not entirely free or that they are blind to their own exploitation.[12] Yet, even if every woman in the pornography industry were participating in it willingly, and even if none were exploited (although neither is true), women could still be harmed by its dissemination. More central to MacKinnon's and Dworkin's discrimination arguments against pornography is the harm it causes to women as a class of people. Pornography portrays women as subordinate to men and identifies their primary purpose as the satisfaction of the sexual desires of men. Such views of women can be adopted by the consumers of pornography and influence how they treat women in their own lives.

The speech that constitutes a hostile work environment is not considered protected by the United States Supreme Court, and this includes the display of pornographic pictures. In *Robinson v. Jacksonville Shipyards, Inc.* (1991) the court ruled that such speech is no different from that used in the commission of other crimes, such as threats or blackmail. While new legislation is required that addresses pornography specifically, it is thought that the speech that causes discrimination outside of the workplace should similarly not be protected. Although the U.S. Supreme Court does not agree, Mackinnon, Dworkin, and many other anti-pornography activists believe that laws against pornography should be able to meet the same First Amendment challenges that Title VII has.

The definition of pornography offered in MacKinnon's model ordinance is "the graphic sexually explicit subordination of women through pictures and words" (MacKinnon, *Feminism Unmodified*, 176); the definition also includes a list of eight features of pornographic films that constitute this subordination, such as presenting women as sexual objects, as victims of violence, and in positions or postures that imply submission or servility. According to MacKinnon, not all sexually explicit material is pornographic. On MacKinnon's account, each of those eight features is a sufficient condition for a sexually explicit film or book being pornographic, although the list is not exhaustive. However, a problem with this definition, as the philosopher Jennifer Saul points out, is with the claim that pornography *is* subordination: "One can understand ... how films or magazines might cause or depict subordination, but it just makes no sense to say that they *are* subordination" (Saul, 227; italics in original). Yet MacKinnon's and Dworkin's arguments for laws against pornography depend on the truth of this claim.

Pornographic pictures in the workplace are prohibited when they are shown to cause the crime of discrimination, but MacKinnon and Dworkin hold that *all* pornography is discriminatory. However, Saul argues, it is difficult, if not impossible, to support the claim that all pornography—that is, all sexually explicit material that depicts women as subordinate—*is* the subordination of women. It might be used to subordinate women, as it is in a hostile environment workplace, but pornography in itself does not do this. For example, it does not do this when it is discussed by Andrea Dworkin in her books, or when pornography is shown at a talk by an anti-pornography activist (Saul, 236). Pornography as it is more typically viewed might have the *effect* of women's subordination by influencing people's views of women (perhaps even if a significant portion of its audience is women). Social scientists and courts have not reached a consensus on whether there is a causal link between pornography and its consumers' views about women, let alone how strong the link might be.[13] However, even if it was shown that there is such a causal connection, it would still not be the case that every instance of pornography had this effect.

The speech that constitutes stranger harassment is similarly not in itself discriminatory, since some of this same speech is used between consensual sexual partners and has other innocuous uses. When such speech occurs in a school or workplace, it contributes to the subordination of women in those particular contexts of power. For it to do so outside of any such specific context a similar disparity in power would have to exist. That is not the case with every instance of stranger harassment unless we hold that the male-dominated nature of society alone provides that disparity. It does not. Even in such a society, not every man is in such a position that an unwelcome sexual communication by him toward a woman is an assertion of his power over her.[14] So there will not always be some individual wielder of power that can be the target of laws and lawsuits against stranger harassment. Stranger harassment resembles hostile environments in workplaces. The federal laws that prohibit such workplace environments in the United States target, correctly, the employers who are responsible for permitting such an environment to flourish and who are thus using their power to enforce this environment upon some of their employees. There is no comparable target for laws aimed at stranger harassment.[15] The law might—and to some extent does—protect women from certain individual instances of stranger harassment. Laws against criminal harassment, disturbing the peace, and assault, for instance, can be used against perpetrators of stranger harassment. The law can do more, but an outright ban on behaviors like catcalls and wolf-whistles would go too far. For example, it would inevitably restrict speech that is not stranger harassment.

In advocating for changes in the law, we need to recognize that any change might affect the application of other laws that we value. For example, combating stranger harassment through the law will inevitably entail limits on speech. This obstacle—if it is found to be insurmountable—does not force us to abandon the cause we are advocating or the other value with which it comes into conflict. The law is not capable of addressing every societal problem, and it is not an appropriate remedy for every such problem. So, for example, someone can believe that pornography portrays women as subordinate, that in doing so it hinders the advancement of women in society or at least reflects views about women that must be abandoned before equality is achieved, but he or she can also believe that there are better and more appropriate ways of combating it than through the law. An analogous position can be taken on stranger harassment. While the law can and does afford some protections to women against stranger harassment, and governments can take other measures to combat it,[16] a more comprehensive legal approach would cause erosion to other rights we value highly.[17]

4. UNDERSTAND THE DIFFICULTIES IN ASSESSING CONSENT

As outlined in Chapter Four, it is not always easy to ascertain the motivations behind the actions of others. While we should not accept wholesale skepticism when it comes to our knowledge of others, we should appreciate that certain contexts make it more difficult to know the thoughts and feelings of others. In our increasingly globalized world, this becomes more difficult because of cultural differences, expressed in language and other behaviors, which sometimes inhibit mutual understanding. These problems are exacerbated in contexts of power where those without power have incentive to conceal or dissimulate their thoughts and feelings.

Failures of mutual understanding can contribute to cases of quid pro quo harassment. For example, a seemingly sincere expression of consent to a sexual relationship might conceal a fear of retaliation. These failures may also play a role in hostile environments. Misunderstanding others can cause us to behave in ways that, unknown to us, are detrimental to the rights and interests of others. Of course, plain indifference to the thoughts and feelings of others is a cause of sexual harassment, as it is in the case of many other harms against individuals.

I discussed above how laws and workplace policies can mandate that we modify our behavior in ways that will prevent sexual harassment. Some of these mandates, if followed, relieve us of the need to understand what is in the minds of others. They prohibit the *types* of behavior that could cause sexual harassment. Some organizations prefer this approach instead of entrusting their members with the responsibility of reasoning about how their behaviors impact others. Rather than leading always to an overly "sanitized workplace" or an unjust constriction of our legal and moral rights, such modifications to our behavior are a common and necessary feature of social life. Some are imposed by others, but most are self-imposed. We behave differently in public than in private and adopt different standards when among colleagues or with close friends or family. We modify our behavior in order to accommodate the rights and interests of others. Nevertheless, there is a legitimate worry that those with authority over us, or our own concerns about interfering in the lives of others, will go too far. The arrangements we make in society to respect and take account of everyone's interests will inevitably be imperfect. Rather than despairing of even trying to balance interests, however, we should allow an awareness of this fact to influence the modifications we impose on our behaviors. For one thing, it should compel us to accept that the arrangements we make will always require adjustment. Our laws and policies should have the flexibility to respond to changing attitudes and circumstances, as well as simply their own failures to alleviate the problems they are meant to address. Absolute prohibitions on such things as inter-office romance lack such flexibility and as such are likely to do more harm than good.

5. APPRECIATE SEXUAL HARASSMENT AS A SERIOUS, PERVASIVE HARM

The most effective motivation for pursuing these recommendations is an appreciation of sexual harassment as a harm that has serious consequences for individuals, businesses and other organizations, as well as society as a whole. These harms are emotional and financial. Victims can experience anger, sadness, shame, and other negative emotions, and these emotional harms are typically manifested in decreased mental or physical health. For instance, victims of sexual harassment can suffer anxiety and depression; such distress can have deleterious effects on physical health, such as weight loss and gastrointestinal problems. The financial harms are felt by both the victim and the organization, since both suffer from the decreased productivity of sexual harassment victims. Organizations lose talent due to sexual harassment. They also suffer the legal costs associated with sexual harassment, not only those that arise when defending themselves against lawsuits, but also in the measures they take to protect themselves from lawsuits, such as developing initiatives against sexual harassment.

Sexual harassment is also a moral wrong with negative consequences for organizations and individuals. As a form of discrimination, it limits the economic and social opportunities of its victims. As an attack on the dignity of its victims, sexual harassment violates a wide spectrum of human rights. All of these harms affect society in general, especially since sexual harassment remains a pervasive problem. Various studies indicate that at least 50 per cent of women have experienced sexual harassment in the workplace or school, and men are increasingly experiencing sexual harassment as well.[18] If we do not take sexual harassment seriously and so do not support such things as workplace initiatives or changes to the law to combat it, we contribute to the problem.

Finally, like most social problems, the causes of sexual harassment run deep in society. Sexual harassment reflects views about the worth of individuals that are so firmly entrenched that it may take generations and more than changes to the law or the policies of organization to eliminate them. Yet these changes and the other recommendations are a first and necessary step to reducing cases of sexual harassment. Combined with other actions, they will eventually help eliminate the views that motivate sexual harassment. That, at least, is their goal.

REVIEW QUESTIONS

1. What are the minimum three components for a complete understanding of sexual harassment?
2. What are the three typical components of an organizational initiative on sexual harassment?
3. What are some of the perceived limits to sexual harassment law?
4. How can failures of mutual understanding cause sexual harassment?
5. What are some of the facts that support the view that sexual harassment is a serious and pervasive harm?

DISCUSSION QUESTIONS

1. In addition to those mentioned in this chapter, what are other ways of promoting an understanding of sexual harassment?
2. Should an organization adopt formal or informal procedures on sexual harassment (or neither)?

3. Is pornography discrimination?
4. Should sexual harassment law be expanded to cover stranger harassment?
5. How should concerns about mutual understanding influence our behavior toward others? Consider the following actions and discuss whether they should be refrained from and, if not absolutely, what sorts of things should be taken into account before they are performed:
    a) Complimenting a co-worker (or a subordinate, student, customer, etc.) on his or her appearance.
    b) Telling a "dirty" joke to a co-worker.
    c) Asking a co-worker on a date.
    d) Sharing one's sexual interests and experiences with a co-worker.
    e) Physically touching a co-worker.

GROUP ACTIVITIES

1. Design a component of a workplace initiative on sexual harassment such as a set of procedures or a training session. Each group can be assigned a different initiative, or several groups can work on versions of one initiative (since a training session has the most content, the activity may focus on just that and each group work on different components of the training). As a full group, present and discuss the initiatives.

2. In discussion with group members, (a) think of ways to expand upon each recommendation in this chapter, and (b) think of other recommendations for preventing sexual harassment. Discuss and evaluate these recommendations in the full group.

NOTES

1 It can be combined with the organization's policy statements on all forms of employment discrimination. There is probably no need to develop separate policies for each form of discrimination. The policy also does not need to be restricted to forms of discrimination recognized by federal law. For example, it can include policy statements against discrimination based on sexual orientation.

2   If the procedure is not centralized in a single office or person (Gutek, 192), those handling the complaint might believe this as well.

3   Research indicates that only 5–18 per cent of female victims of sexual harassment report it to authorities in the workplace (Sbraga and O'Donohue).

4   Interestingly, in both studies, the effects of training were larger and/or only significant for the male trainees.

5   Consultants and law firms are doing estimated billions of dollars of business advising companies on how to prevent sexual harassment, including providing anti-harassment training (see Stuart Silverstein, "Fear of Lawsuits Spurs the Birth of New Industry," *Los Angeles Times* 27 June 1998: A1).

6   Maine requires training of all employees in a business. In New Jersey, the state Supreme Court mandates the training (*Gaines v. Bellino*, 173 N.J. 301 [2002]); in the other states, legislation requires it.

7   Susan Bisom-Rapp worries that ineffective training programs might still create "the illusion that discrimination is being meaningfully addressed" (Bisom-Rapp, 45). She recommends that courts not automatically accept the existence of a training program as evidence that an employer is serious about eliminating discrimination. She also believes that more research needs to be done on the effectiviness of anti-discrimination training programs generally before courts and the legal profession fully accept them as a preventive measure.

8   Not all harassment is discriminatory, and not all of it is sexual. Ehrenreich's approach aims to provide legal protections to all victims of workplace harassment. It is also compatible with her dignity theory approach to sexual harassment, which was discussed in Chapter Two. It is an approach rejected by MacKinnon as a means of addressing sexual harassment (see MacKinnon, *Sexual Harassment*, 164–74).

9   In many U.S. states, citizens elect their state Supreme Court justices, who then interpret state sexual harassment law.

10   Books by MacKinnon and Dworkin relevant to the topic of pornography include Dworkin, *Pornography*; MacKinnon, *Feminism Unmodified*, *Toward a Feminist Theory of the State*, and *Only Words*; and Dworkin and MacKinnon.

11   *R. v. Butler*, [1992] 1 S.C.R. 452.

12   See Caroline West's *Stanford Encyclopedia of Philosophy* entry on "Pornography and Censorship" (see Appendix B) for some discussion of this and other very useful information on the pornography and free speech debate.

13   Pornography certainly reflects certain views about women, and it can in some way help sustain those views. It is certainly false that pornography alone is responsible for these views, and it might be the case that those who consume pornography (that is, sexually explicit material that portrays women as subordinate) do so because they already hold these views; it is not pornography that causes them to hold these views.

14   Consider again the case of Marie from Chapter Three. The unwelcome sexual communications directed at her from the men at the construction site might contribute to some degree to overall male power. However, those men are not necessarily asserting any power over Marie. This is clearly the case if, for example, Marie—let us say unbeknownst to them—is the owner of the building they are constructing. She would have more relative power, for example, the power to get them fired, along with various other powers associated with her higher economic class.

15   Male-dominated society is not the sort of entity that can be a target of this or any other law. However, one possible legal means for curtailing some cases of stranger harassment is directing these laws against the employers of those who are committing the stranger harassment, e.g., the construction company that hires the men who direct catcalls at the women that pass by. Current anti-discrimination laws govern businesses' treatment of their clients or customers. To change the law in the suggested way would entail overseeing their relations with everyone else. Such a law would hold employers vicariously liable for more of their employees' behavior. One effect would be increased surveillance of employees; employee privacy would then become an issue.

16   For example, Fairchild and Rudman report on the governments in Tokyo and Rio de Janeiro designating certain subway cars women-only during rush hour to reduce incidents of stranger harassment of women (Fairchild and Rudman, 339).

17   Examples of alternatives to government approaches include the website ihollaback.org. Founded in 2005, the website collects and posts reports of street harassment from women around the world. It also offers applications for mobile devices that allow for immediate reporting and posting of incidents of harassment.

18   See the Introduction for these and other statistics on the prevalence and effects of sexual harassment.

Appendix A: Legal Definitions of Sexual Harassment

Equal Employment Opportunity Commission
Unwelcome sexual advances, requests for sexual favors, and other verbal or physical conduct of a sexual nature constitute sexual harassment when (1) submission to such conduct is made either explicitly or implicitly a term or condition of an individual's employment, (2) submission to or rejection of such conduct by an individual is used as the basis for employment decisions affecting such individual, or (3) such conduct has the purpose or effect of unreasonably interfering with an individual's work performance or creating an intimidating, hostile, or offensive working environment.[1]

Office of Civil Rights at the U.S. Department of Education
Sexual harassment can take two forms: quid pro quo and hostile environment.

Quid pro quo harassment occurs when a school employee causes a student to believe that he or she must submit to unwelcome sexual conduct in order to participate in a school program or activity. It can also occur when an employee causes a student to believe that the employee will make an educational decision based on whether or not the student submits to unwelcome sexual conduct. For example, when a teacher threatens to fail a student unless the student agrees to date the teacher, it is quid pro quo harassment.

Hostile environment harassment occurs when unwelcome conduct of a sexual nature is so severe, persistent, or pervasive that it affects a student's ability to participate in or benefit from an education program or activity, or creates an intimidating, threatening or abusive educational environment. A hostile environment can be created by a school employee, another student, or even someone visiting the school, such as a student or employee from another school.[2]

Canada Labour Code

... "sexual harassment" means any conduct, comment, gesture or contact of a sexual nature

a) that is likely to cause offence or humiliation to any employee;
   or
b) that might, on reasonable grounds, be perceived by
   that employee as placing a condition of a sexual nature
   on employment or on any opportunity for training or
   promotion.[3]

European Union

[Sexual harassment is] unwanted conduct of a sexual nature, or other conduct based on sex affecting the dignity of women and men at work. This includes unwelcome physical, verbal or nonverbal conduct.

Conduct is considered sexual harassment if it is (1) unwanted, improper or offensive; (2) if the victim's refusal or acceptance of the behavior influences decisions concerning her employment or (3) the conduct creates an intimidating, hostile or humiliating working environment for the recipient.[4]

Australia

... a person sexually harasses another person ... if: (a) the person makes an unwelcome sexual advance, or an unwelcome request for sexual favours, to the person harassed; or (b) engages in other unwelcome conduct of a sexual nature in relation to the person harassed; in circumstances in which a reasonable person, having regard to all the circumstances, would have anticipated that the person harassed would be offended, humiliated or intimidated.... In this section: "*conduct of a sexual nature*" includes making a statement of a sexual nature to a person, or in the presence of a person, whether the statement is made orally or in writing.[5]

United Nations

Sexual harassment includes such unwelcome sexually determined behaviour as physical contact and advances, sexually coloured remarks, showing pornography and sexual demands, whether by words or actions. Such conduct can be humiliating and may constitute a health and safety problem; it is discriminatory when the woman has reasonable ground to believe that her objection would disadvantage her in connection with her employment, including recruitment or promotion, or when it creates a hostile working environment.[6]

NOTES

1 Code of Federal Regulations: Title 29, Sec. 1604.11.
2 <http://www2.ed.gov/about/offices/list/ocr/qa-sexharass.html>; accessed 5 July 2010.
3 Part III, Division XV.1.
4 European Union Commission Recommendation 92/131/EEC of 27 November 1991: 2.
5 Sex Discrimination Act of 1984, Section 28A.
6 Committee on the Elimination of Discrimination against Women, General Recommendation 19, Violence against Women (Eleventh session, 1992), U.N. Doc. A/47/38 at 1 (1993).

Appendix B: Websites

GOVERNMENT ORGANIZATIONS

Equal Employment Opportunity Commission
<http://www.eeoc.gov>

Canadian Human Rights Commission
<http://www.chrc-ccdp.ca>

Canadian Human Rights Tribunal
<http://www.chrt-tcdp.gc.ca>

Office of Civil Rights at the U.S. Department of Education
<http://www2.ed.gov/about/offices/list/ocr/>

Civil Rights Division of the U. S. Department of Justice
<http://www.justice.gov/crt/>

PROFESSIONAL ORGANIZATIONS

American Psychological Association
<http://www.apa.org/ethics/code/index.aspx>

American Bar Association
<http://www.abanet.org/cpr/mrpc/model_rules.html>

American Medical Association
<http://www.ama-assn.org/ama/pub/physician-resources/medical-ethics.shtml>

American Association of University Professors
<http://www.aaup.org/AAUP/pubsres/policydocs/contents/sexharass.htm>

The Canadian Bar Association
<http://www.cba.org>

MISCELLANEOUS

Stanford Encyclopedia of Philosophy
<http://www.plato.stanford.edu>

Society for Business Ethics
<http://www.societyforbusinessethics.org>

Association for Practical and Professional Ethics
<http://www.indiana.edu/~appe>

National Organization for Women
<http://www.now.org/issues/harass/>

Feminist Majority Foundation
<http://www.feminist.org/911/harass.html>

National Women's Law Center
<http://www.nwlc.org>

American Association of University Women
<http://www.aauw.org/act/laf/library/harassment.cfm>

Stop Street Harassment
<http://www.stopstreetharassment.org>

Appendix C: Sexual Harassment in Film and Television

Disclosure (1994)
Based on a bestselling novel by Michael Crichton, a thriller about a man (Michael Douglas) who sues his boss (Demi Moore) for sexual harassment. Initially, his wife and co-workers have trouble under-standing how he could be a victim of sexual harassment. At one point, in trying to explain this to his wife, he says, "Sexual harassment is about power. When did I have the power?" He also has to contend with retaliation by his boss.

Disgrace (2008)
Based on a novel of the same name by Nobel-prize-winning author J.M. Coetzee, set in South Africa, it is the story of a professor (John Malkovich) who seduces a student, is forced to resign his position, and moves to the country to live with his daughter. Initially unrepen-tant, a tragic event leads him to re-evaluate his past actions.

Family Guy: "I am Peter, Hear Me Roar" (2000)
Peter is sued for sexual harassment and forced to attend sensitivity training.

Family Guy: "Peter-assment" (2010)
Peter is sexually harassed by his new female boss.

Female (1933)
The female president of an automobile company (Ruth Chatterton) enjoys sleeping with male subordinates and then transferring them when she is done with them.

Hostile Advances: The Kerry Ellison Story (1996)
A television movie about the plaintiff in *Ellison v. Brady* (1991), the case that established the "reasonable woman" standard.

In the Company of Men (1997)
Two business executives (Aaron Eckhart and Matt Malloy) attempt revenge against all the women who have slighted them by trying separately to romance a co-worker, cause her to fall in love with one of them, and then immediately dump her when she does. They choose a young deaf woman (Stacy Edwards), who holds a lower-level position in their company, and one of them succeeds with the plan.

The Magdalene Sisters (2002)
Inspired by true events, the story of inmates at a Magdalene Laundry (institutions for "fallen women" that existed in Europe and North America until the late twentieth century) in Ireland who suffered physical, emotional, and sexual abuse at the hands of their nun and priest warders.

Nine to Five (1980)
Dolly Parton, Jane Fonda, and Lily Tomlin play office workers who enact revenge on their sexually harassing boss.

North Country (2005)
Starring Charlize Theron, a fictionalized account of the events that led to the first class-action sexual harassment lawsuit, *Jenson v. Eveleth*

Taconite Co. (1988); it was filed by woman miners in Minnesota who endured a hostile work environment. Their stories are also chronicled in the 2002 book *Class Action: The Story of Lois Jenson and the Landmark Case that Changed Sexual Harassment Law,* by Clara Bingham and Laura Leedy Gansler.

The Office: "Sexual Harassment" (2005)
Inappropriate behavior by the boss Michael requires that the entire staff undergo a review of the company's sexual harassment policy. Michael's behavior remains a model of hostile environment through most of the series.

Oleanna (1994)
David Mamet's adaptation of his own play; it includes only two characters: a professor (William H. Macy) and the student (Debra Eisenstadt) who accuses him of sexual harassment. The sexual harassment is supposed to have occurred in the first act of the movie; in the movie's second and final act the two confront each other over their different interpretations of what happened.

Pretty Persuasion (2005)
A comedy about a manipulative aspiring actress (Evan Rachel Wood) who leads a group of girls at a private high school in Beverly Hills that accuse their teacher of sexual harassment.

Secretary (2002)
Based on a short story by Mary Gaitskill, a dark comedy about a sado-masochistic sexual relationship between an attorney (James Spader) and his secretary (Maggie Gyllenhaal).

The Simpsons: "Homer Badman" (1994)
Homer is mistakenly accused of sexual harassment by a college-aged babysitter.

South Park: "Sexual Harassment Panda" (1999)
The Sexual Harassment Panda visits the boys' school to deliver a training session (with visual aids and a song) on sexual harassment; it inspires Cartman to sue Stan for sexual harassment.

Strange Justice (1999)
A television movie about the events surrounding Anita Hill's accusations of sexual harassment against Clarence Thomas during his confirmation hearings for the United States Supreme Court; based on the book of the same name by Jane Mayer and Jill Abramson.

Glossary

at-will doctrine legal doctrine which holds that employees not hired under a contract can be fired for a good reason, no reason, or even a bad reason; at-will employees have reciprocal rights to quit for any reason.

Canadian Human Rights Commission charged with investigating complaints of discrimination according to the 1977 Canadian Human Rights Act.

coercion compelling another person to perform some action by threatening to bring about something that they find less desirable than performing that action.

dignity theories a collection of theories that see the primary harm of sexual harassment to be an attack on a person's rights and other characteristics that constitute his or her dignity.

Equal Employment Opportunity Commission the U.S. governmental body responsible for enforcing anti-discrimination laws, including Title VII of the Civil Rights Act of 1964, which covers sexual harassment.

equality theories a collection of theories that see the primary harm of sexual harassment to be discrimination.

equal-opportunity harasser also known as the "bisexual harasser," a harasser whose victims are both men and women.

family resemblance concept a concept that cannot be defined in terms of necessary and sufficient conditions; the term was coined by the philosopher Ludwig Wittgenstein.

fraternization prohibited relationships within the military; covers various kinds of relationships including romantic or sexual relationships between officers and enlisted personnel.

hostile environment one of the two commonly recognized types of sexual harassment (for the other, see "quid pro quo"); it occurs when there is repeated and pervasive discriminatory behavior or practices within a workplace or school, such as degrading sexual remarks, display of pornographic pictures, unwelcome physical contact, and so on.

quid pro quo one of the two commonly recognized types of sexual harassment (for the other, see "hostile environment"); it occurs when a person demands of someone over whom he or she has power sexual favors in exchange for some employment or academic benefit.

reasonable woman standard a standard employed in judicial decision making that involves looking at a situation from the perspective of a hypothetical "reasonable woman" in order to determine whether a hostile environment exists; the standard is meant to take into account differences between the perspectives of men and women.

same-sex sexual harassment a case of sexual harassment in which the harasser and the victim are of the same gender.

stranger harassment unwanted sexual attention from strangers in public places.

third-party employees employees who are not the direct targets of sexually harassing behavior, but who are nevertheless harmed by the behavior.

vicarious liability the liability of employers for sexual harassment by their employees, even when the employers were not directly involved in the harassment.

References

Adams, Jann H. "Sexual Harassment and Black Women: A Historical Perspective." *Sexual Harassment: Theory, Research, and Treatment.* Ed. William O'Donohue. Boston: Allyn and Bacon, 1997. 213–24.

American Association of University Women. *Hostile Hallways: Bullying, Teasing, and Sexual Harassment in School.* Washington, DC: American Association of University Women Educational Foundation, 2001.

Anderson, Elizabeth. "Recent Thinking about Sexual Harassment: A Review Essay." *Philosophy & Public Affairs* 34.3 (2006): 284–311.

Antecol, Heather, and Deborah Cobb-Clark. "Does Sexual Harassment Change Attitudes? A View from the Federal Level." *Social Science Quarterly* 84.4 (2003): 826–42.

Baer, Susanne. "Dignity or Equality? Responses to Workplace Harassment in European, German, and U.S. Law." *Directions in Sexual Harassment Law.* Ed. Catharine A. MacKinnon and Reva B. Siegel. New Haven, CT: Yale University Press, 2004. 582–601.

Baker, Carrie N. *The Women's Movement Against Sexual Harassment.* New York: Cambridge University Press, 2008.

Bayles, Michael. "Coercive Offers and Public Benefits." *The Personalist* 55.2 (1974): 139–44.

Bisom-Rapp, Susan. "An Ounce of Prevention is a Poor Substitute for a Pound of Cure: Confronting the Developing Jurisprudence of Education and Prevention in Employment Discrimination Law." *Berkeley Journal of Employment and Labor Law* 22.1 (2001): 1–47.

Browne, Kingsley R. "Title VII as Censorship: Hostile-Environment Harassment and the First Amendment." *Ohio State Law Journal* 52 (1991): 481–550.

Conte, Alba. "Legal Theories of Sexual Harassment." *Sexual Harassment: Theory, Research, and Treatment*. Ed. William O'Donohue. Boston: Allyn and Bacon, 1997. 50–83.

Crosthwaite, Jan, and Graham Priest. "The Definition of Sexual Harassment." *Sexual Harassment: Issues and Answers*. Ed. Linda LeMoncheck and James Sterba. New York: Oxford University Press, 2001. 62–77.

Crouch, Margaret. *Thinking About Sexual Harassment: A Guide for the Perplexed*. New York: Oxford University Press, 2001.

Dodds, Susan M., Lucy Frost, Robert Pargetter, and Elizabeth W. Prior. "Sexual Harassment." *Social Theory and Practice* 14 (1988): 111–30.

Dolezalek, H. "2005 Industry Report." *Training* 41.12 (2005): 14–28.

Dromm, Keith. "The Hostile Office: Michael as a Sexual Harasser." *The Office and Philosophy*. Ed. J. Jeremy Wisnewski. Oxford: Blackwell, 2008. 193–206.

Dworkin, Andrea. *Intercourse*. New York: Basic Books, 2007.

——. *Pornography: Men Possessing Women*. New York: Plume, 1979.

——, and Catharine MacKinnon. *Pornography and Civil Rights: A New Day*. Minneapolis: Organizing against Pornography, 1988.

Ehrenreich, Rosa. "Dignity and Discrimination: Toward a Pluralistic Understanding of Workplace Harassment." *The Georgetown Law Journal* 88.1 (1999): 1–64.

Fairchild, Kimberly, and Laurie A. Rudman. "Everyday Stranger Harassment and Women's Objectification." *Social Justice Research* 21 (2008): 338–57.

Faley, Robert H., Deborah Erdos Knapp, Gary A. Kustis, and Cathy L.Z. Dubois, "Estimating the Organizational Costs of Sexual Harassment: The Case of the U.S. Army." *Journal of Business and Psychology* 13 (1999): 461–84.

Feary, Vaughana Macy. "Sexual Harassment: Why the Corporate World Still Doesn't 'Get It.'" *Journal of Business Ethics* 13 (1994): 649–62.

Franke, Katherine M. "What's Wrong with Sexual Harassment." *Stanford Law Review* 49.4 (1997): 691–772.

Gallop, Jane. *Feminist Accused of Sexual Harassment*. Durham, NC: Duke University Press, 1997.

Gruber, James. "Sexual Harassment in the Public Sector." *Academic and Workplace Sexual Harassment*. Ed. Michele Paludi and Carman A. Paludi, Jr. Westport, CT: Praeger, 2003. 49–75.

Gutek, Barbara. "Sexual Harassment Policy Initiatives." *Sexual Harassment: Theory, Research, and Treatment*. Ed. William O'Donohue. Needham Heights, MA: Allyn & Bacon, 1997. 185–98.

Hill, Catherine, and Holly Kearl. *Crossing the Line: Sexual Harassment at School*. Washington, DC: American Association of University Women Educational Foundation, 2011.

Hill, Catherine, and Elena Silva. *Drawing the Line: Sexual Harassment on Campus*. Washington, DC: American Association of University Women Educational Foundation, 2005.

Ilies, R., N. Hauserman, S. Schwochau, and J. Stibal, "Reported Incidence Rates of Work-Related Sexual Harassment in the

United States: Using Meta-Analysis to Explain Reported Rate Disparities." *Personnel Psychology* 56 (2003): 607–31.

Kamir, Orit. "Dignity, Respect, and Equality in Israel's Sexual Harassment Law." *Directions in Sexual Harassment Law*. Ed. Catharine A. MacKinnon and Reva B. Siegel. New Haven, CT: Yale University Press, 2004. 561–81.

Kirshenbaum, Andrea Meryl. "'Because of ... Sex': Rethinking the Protections Afforded under Title VII in the Post-Onacle World." *Albany Law Review* 69 (2005): 139–77.

Landau, Iddo. "Sexual Harassment and the 'Repetition Requirement.'" *Philosophy of the Social Sciences* 34.1 (2004): 79–83.

——. "Sexual Harassment as 'Wrongful Communication.'" *Philosophy of the Social Sciences* 33.2 (2003): 225–34.

Leeser, Jaimie, and William O'Donohue. "Normative Issues in Defining Sexual Harassment." *Sexual Harassment: Theory, Research, and Treatment*. Ed. William O'Donohue. Boston: Allyn and Bacon, 1997. 29–49.

LeMoncheck, Linda, and James P. Sterba. *Sexual Harassment: Issues and Answers*. New York: Oxford University Press, 2001.

Levitsky, Sandra. "Closing the 'Bisexual Defense' Loophole in Title VII Sexual Harassment Cases." *Sexual Harassment: Issues and Answers*. Ed. Linda LeMoncheck and James Sterba. New York: Oxford University Press, 2001. 214–28.

Lundberg-Love, Paula, and Shelly Marmion. "Sexual Harassment in the Private Sector." *Academic and Workplace Sexual Harassment*. Ed. Michele Paludi and Carmen A. Paludi, Jr. Westport, CT: Praeger, 2003. 77–101.

MacKinnon, Catharine A. *Feminism Unmodified*. Cambridge, MA: Harvard University Press, 1987.

——. *Only Words*. Cambridge, MA: Harvard University Press, 1993.

——. *Sexual Harassment of Working Women: A Case of Sex Discrimination*. New Haven, CT: Yale University Press, 1979.

——. *Toward a Feminist Theory of the State*. Cambridge, MA: Harvard University Press, 1989.

——, and Reva B. Siegel. *Directions in Sexual Harassment Law*. New Haven, CT: Yale University Press, 2004.

Macmillan, Ross, Annette Nierobisz, and Sandy Welsh. "Experiencing the Streets: Harassment and Perceptions of Safety Among Women." *Journal of Research in Crime and Delinquency* 37 (2000): 306–22.

Martucci, William C., and Zheng Lu. "Sexual-Harassment Training: The Wave of the Future in State Legislative Efforts." *Employment Relations Today* 32.2 (2005): 87–95.

Moyer, Robert S., and Anjan Nath. "Some Effects of Brief Training Interventions on Perceptions of Sexual Harassment." *Journal of Applied Social Psychology* 28.4 (1998): 333–56.

Murray, Sandra L., John G. Holmes, and Dale W. Griffin. "The Benefits of Positive Illusions: Idealization and the Construction of Satisfaction in Close Relationships." *Journal of Personality and Social Psychology* 70.1 (1996): 79–98.

Nozick, Robert. "Coercion." *Philosophy, Science, and Method*. Ed. Sidney Morgenbesser, Patrick Suppes, and Morton White. New York: St. Martin's Press, 1969. 440–72.

O'Donohue, William, ed. *Sexual Harassment: Theory, Research, and Treatment*. Boston: Allyn and Bacon, 1997.

Oppenheimer, David B. "Employer Liability for Sexual Harassment by Supervisors." *Directions in Sexual Harassment Law*. Ed. Catharine A. MacKinnon and Reva B. Siegel. New Haven, CT: Yale University Press, 2004. 272–89.

Perry, Elissa L., Carol T. Kulik, and Marina P. Field. "Sexual Harassment Training: Recommendations to Address Gaps between the Practitioner and Research Literatures." *Human Resource Management* 48.5 (2009): 817–37.

Perry, Elissa L., Carol T. Kulik, Jennifer Bustamante, and Frank D. Golom, "The Impact of Reason for Training on the Relationship Between 'Best Practices' and Sexual Harassment Training Effectiveness." *Human Resource Development Quarterly* 21.2 (2010): 187–208.

Plato. *The Dialogues of Plato*. Trans. B. Jowett. Oxford: Clarendon Press, 1871.

———. *Symposium*. Trans. Alexander Nehamas and Paul Woodruff. Indianapolis: Hackett, 1989.

Ryle, Gilbert. *The Concept of Mind*. Chicago: University of Chicago Press, 1984.

Saguy, Abigail C. "French and American Lawyers Define Sexual Harassment." *Directions in Sexual Harassment Law*. Ed. Catharine A. MacKinnon and Reva B. Siegel. New Haven, CT: Yale University Press, 2004. 602–17.

Saul, Jennifer. "Pornography, Speech Acts and Context." *Proceedings of the Aristotelian Society* 106.2 (2006): 227–46.

Sbraga, Tamara Penix, and William O'Donohue. "Sexual Harassment." *Annual Review of Sex Research* (2000): 258–85.

Schultz, Vicki. "The Sanitized Workplace." *Yale Law Journal* 112 (2003): 2061–2193.

Segrave, Kerry. *The Sexual Harassment of Women in the Workplace, 1600 to 1993*. Jefferson, NC: McFarland & Company, 1994.

Siegel, Reva B. "Introduction: A Short History of Sexual Harassment." *Directions in Sexual Harassment Law*. Ed. Catharine A. MacKinnon and Reva B. Siegel. New Haven, CT: Yale University Press, 2004. 1–39.

Simon, Anne E. "Alexander v. Yale University: An Informal History." *Directions in Sexual Harassment Law*. Ed. Catharine A. MacKinnon and Reva B. Siegel. New Haven, CT: Yale University Press, 2004. 51–59.

Sogunro, Olusegun Agboola. "Efficacy of Role-Playing Pedagogy in Training Leaders: Some Reflections." *Journal of Management Development* 23.4 (2004): 355–71.

Stendhal. *On Love.* Trans. H.B.V. New York: Liveright, 1947.

Sterba, James P. "Understanding, Explaining, and Eliminating Sexual Harassment." *Sexual Harassment: Issues and Answers.* Ed. Linda LeMoncheck and James P. Sterba. New York: Oxford University Press, 2001. 231–44.

Superson, Anita. "A Feminist Definition of Sexual Harassment." *Journal of Social Philosophy* 24 (1993): 46–64.

Tuana, Nancy. "Sexual Harassment in Academe: Issues of Power and Coercion." *Sexual Harassment: Confrontations and Decisions.* Ed. Edmund Wall. Buffalo, NY: Prometheus Books, 1992. 48–60.

——. "Sexual Harassment: Offers and Coercion." *Journal of Social Philosophy* 19.2 (1988): 30–42.

Uggen, Christopher, and Chika Shinohara. "Sexual Harassment Comes of Age: A Comparative Analysis of the United States and Japan." *The Sociological Quarterly* 50 (2009): 201–34.

Vander Velde, Lea. "Coercion in At-Will Employment and Sexual Harassment." *Directions in Sexual Harassment Law.* Ed. Catharine A. MacKinnon and Reva B. Siegel. New Haven, CT: Yale University Press, 2004. 496–515.

Wall, Edmund. "The Definition of Sexual Harassment." *Sexual Harassment: Confrontations and Decisions.* Ed. Edmund Wall. Buffalo: Prometheus Books, 1992. 69–85.

——. "Reply to Iddo Landau." *Philosophy of the Social Sciences* 33.2 (2003): 235–41.

——. "Sexual Harassment and Wrongful Communication." *Philosophy of the Social Sciences* 31.4 (2001): 525–37.

Wesselmann, Eric D., and Janice R. Kelly. "Cat-Calls and Culpability: Investigating the Frequency and Functions of Stranger Harassment." *Sex Roles* 63 (2010): 451–62.

Willness, Chelsea R., Piers Steel, and Kibeom Lee. "A Meta-Analysis of the Antecedents and Consequences of Workplace Sexual Harassment." *Personnel Psychology* 60 (2007): 127–62.

Wittgenstein, Ludwig. *Philosophical Investigations*. Trans. G.E.M. Anscombe, P.M.S. Hacker, and Joachim Schulte. Oxford: Wiley-Blackwell, 2009.

Zimmerman, David. "Coercive Wage Offers." *Philosophy & Public Affairs* 10.2 (1981): 121–45.

Index

LIST
of products used:

549 lb(s) of Rolland Enviro100 Print
100% post-consumer

RESULTS
Based on the Cascades products you selected
compared to products in the industry made with
100% virgin fiber, your savings are:

 5 trees

 4,542 gal. US of water
49 days of water consumption

574 lbs of waste
5 waste containers

 1,492 lbs CO2
2,830 miles driven

7 MMBTU
35,396 60W light bulbs for one hour

4 lbs NOX
**emissions of one truck during 6
days**